Just Watch the Game (Again)

Just Watch The Game. (Again)

John Steigerwald

Published by
Little M Productions
Canonsburg, PA 15317

Paperback ISBN: 978-1-4507-9195-3

Cover design by Eric Hammond Subcreations

Printed in the United States of America

Contents

*This book is dedicated to Emma, Gunnar,
Jake, Katie, Luke and Wyatt.*

FOREWORD

After further review, everything I wrote in my first book stands. I can't believe I just wrote a sentence that contains the words "in my first book."

I never thought I would write a book and here I am with book Number 2. Believe it or not, in 2010 lots of people actually bought "Just Watch the Game." So, I figured if you can fool 'em once....

In case you were among the millions who didn't read "Just Watch the Game," the title comes from my dad. When he would catch me spending too much time looking for the popcorn vendor at Forbes Field during a Pirates game, he would give me a nudge, gesture toward the field and say, "Just watch the game."

I thought that was a perfect title for my book because that's all I really ever wanted to do while covering sports for almost 40 years. I've enjoyed the access that I've had to the players and the other perks, but I became a sportscaster because I couldn't imagine any job that could be better than being paid to watch games.

And it took writing "Just Watch the Game" for me to realize just how interesting my life has been. Spending a day flying to and from a golf tournament with Arnold Palmer or covering a World Series with Bob Prince sure beats the hell out of sitting in a cubicle counting the minutes until lunchtime every day.

Chapter 20 in "Just Watch the Game (Again)" is called "I Wish I Had Known." It's my way of publicly kicking myself for not being smart enough to know that all the interesting things I was experiencing and people I was meeting would make a pretty good book some day.

I never lost sight of how lucky I was to have the job that I had. Or how lucky I was to have it in a town that produced so many great teams and memorable personalities. So it wasn't a case of not stopping to smell the roses. It was more of a case of not stopping to take notes.

As it turned out, I was able to crank out what I think are two pretty good books. It's just that I know they could have been a lot better if only I had known I was going to write them.

For example, I sure as hell didn't know, when I was in the fifth grade at St. Bernard's school in Mt. Lebanon, that my experiences trying to hide my uneaten stewed tomatoes from dreaded Sister Mary Flavia, the Holy Troll of the Cafeteria, would make it into a book. You'll be introduced to Sister Flavia in Chapter 36, the story of a local grade school football team that lost three games in 13 years.

You don't need to take notes when you get a chance to play right field in a Pirates spring training intrasquad game. That experience is going to stick with you and I remember it like it was yesterday. Fortunately for me, Chuck Tanner was the manager and you'll see in Chapter 6 that he and a major technical problem with a camera played a role in making the story 10 times more interesting and memorable.

My yearning for the days when just watching the game was enough provided the impetus to write a successful book. But it also got me a ticket to Cyber Hell when I questioned the judgment of a 42-year-old father of two who ended up with severe brain damage and in a coma when he was beaten for wearing a Giants jersey to a Dodgers game. In Chapter 5 you get my firsthand account of what it was like to hold the title of "Most Hated Man in America." If everybody who trashed me on the Internet buys this book, you're reading a million-seller.

Ninety-nine percent of the baseball fans on Earth will tell you that it's a slam-dunk that Barry Bonds was a better player than Roberto Clemente. In Chapter 8, I say not necessarily and I have some numbers to back up my argument.

How many times have you seen the film of Bill Mazeroski's 1960 World Series home run? In Chapter 28, "Behind the Scores (Literally)," you'll get a totally different perspective on Maz's home run from a guy who was looking into Yankee leftfielder Yogi Berra's eyes as he watched the ball barely clear the ivy-covered wall.

There are lots of other ramblings, reminiscences and revelations.

In "You Can't Care More Than Your Boss," I tell a story about a TV story that I didn't do in 2001. I tell you why the fact that my boss at KDKA didn't think it was worth covering convinced me that local television news had officially become a joke — seven years before I stopped working in it.

It may surprise you to find out that Pittsburgh's baddest-man-ever didn't play for the Steelers and his highlights have never been seen on ESPN, but he's in this book too.

I even have answers to questions that you may not have asked yourself. Such as, how did Dave Parker get the nickname "Cobra" and why was he the most underrated and underappreciated athlete in Pittsburgh sports history? And what was going through a local guy's mind when he was a couple of hours away from having been on the wrong end of one of the biggest upsets in boxing history? And who the hell was Co Prins and how did he get in this book?

It's all in here – and more. And the best part is you don't have to read the chapters in order. I was told that "Just Watch the Game" was a great book to keep in the bathroom. I can't think of a better compliment and I can only hope that this book ends up there too.

CHAPTER I

YOU DON'T HAVE THE "T"

I used to work with Terry Bradshaw.

He and I were both working for KDKA in 1986, I as a sports anchor/ reporter and he as a long-distance Steelers analyst. Bradshaw, who had been retired for three years but was still a bigger deal than anybody on the 1986 Steelers, was working as a CBS analyst and KDKA was (and still is) a CBS affiliate, so it was a perfect match.

I knew that Bradshaw would be a big star in TV long before he retired from football. He was a natural because he had an appealing personality and he knew how to bring that to television. He had discovered the simple secret that so many failed aspirants to a TV career have never discovered.

The ability and — more important — the confidence and willingness to be himself.

Remember, this was a guy who was ridiculed for many years for being "dumb" because of his Louisiana drawl. Back then, as now, Pittsburghers weren't aware that nobody from Pittsburgh has the right to make fun of the way anybody else talks.

Bradshaw was smart enough to act just dumb enough to appeal to the people who were dumb enough not to realize how smart he was.

You don't last as long as he has in the network television business if you're not smart.

Bradshaw was hired (the figure I always heard but never had confirmed was $50,000) to appear every Monday during Steelers season to do a live analysis of the previous day's Steelers game.

But he didn't do it from the KDKA studios in Pittsburgh.

He did it from a satellite studio near his home on the outskirts of Dallas.

That's what made it such an adventure. The plan was for KDKA to airmail a videotape of the game to Dallas and have it delivered to Bradshaw's home in time for him to watch it before his appearance on the KDKA Monday 6 o'clock news.

Bradshaw was working as a color analyst on CBS Sunday telecasts and rarely saw the Steelers play. Of course, there was no Internet and no YouTube, so the tapes could only be physically delivered.

You can imagine the adventure that created.

I can recall sitting in the sports seat on the KDKA news set four or five minutes before Bradshaw was supposed to appear by satellite. I would be watching the monitor in the studio to see when Bradshaw arrived, sat down in his chair and had his earpiece put in and his microphone attached.

Virtually all of our five- or six-minute sportscast on Monday was dedicated to the Bradshaw interview, so if anything would go wrong with the feed we would be stuck with all that time to fill.

It usually went like this:

THREE MINUTES TO AIR

Through my studio mic, I ask producer Bruce Shepman, "Where is he."

Bruce: "No idea." Bradshaw didn't have a car phone.

Me: "Do you know if he had a chance to see the game?"

Bruce: "No idea."

TWO MINUTES TO AIR

Still no Bradshaw. We're in commercial break and I'm sitting in front of the camera looking at a monitor with a shot of an empty chair.

Me: "Any sign of him?"

Bruce: "Nope."

A MINUTE AND A HALF TO AIR

The chair is still empty.

Bruce: "He's coming in the door."

Me: "Do you know if he watched the tape?"

Bruce: "No idea, I'll ask him when he's hooked up."

ONE MINUTE TO AIR

I see in the monitor that Bradshaw has his earpiece in, and I hear him say to Bruce, "I didn't see the game, tell me what happened."

Bruce would use the remaining 45 seconds to fill Bradshaw in on what happened in the Steelers game and suggest some topics for him to cover while I began the sports segment.

Me: "The Steelers lost to the Bengals yesterday and blah, blah, blah … let's go live now to Terry Bradshaw in Dallas for some analysis."

We would do the interview and Bradshaw would earn every nickel KDKA was paying him. No one would ever have known that he hadn't seen a minute of the Steelers game.

That wasn't how it went down every week, but it happened more often than not.

He got away with it by the force of his personality.

It didn't bother me because I was thrilled to have him on our air and I'm sure KDKA's 6 o'clock ratings made him worth every cent.

A few weeks into the season, the decision was made to send me, Bruce Shepman and photographer Michael Challik to Dallas to spend some time with Bradshaw at his home.

I don't remember a lot about his home except that it sat on a lot of land, it was beautiful and it was big. When we pulled up to his property, Bradshaw was fishing off one of the decks near his private fishing hole.

We went inside and I did a long interview with him sitting on a big couch in his big great room. During part of the interview in the middle of all that bigness, Bradshaw was holding his tiny dog — a miniature dachshund.

Challik wanted to get some B-roll to cover the interview, so he asked Terry and me to go outside and throw a football back and forth for a while.

That was interesting because Bradshaw had retired after the 1983 season because of a sore arm and nobody had really seen him throw.

He still had the touch.

I was about 45 yards away and running "out" patterns to the railroad ties holding up the top tier of his lawn. The railroad tie was the sideline and I was doing my best to plant both feet in bounds just short of it as the passes would come.

Time after time, Bradshaw would flick his wrist and the ball would land in my hands just as my feet were landing "in bounds" next to the railroad tie.

It made for good B-roll but it also gave me an opening to ask him a question that I had always wanted to ask.

"How the hell can you throw a football with your index finger resting directly on the point of the ball?"

That always amazed me because I had never seen anybody throw a football better than Bradshaw (still haven't) and I had never seen another quarterback grip the ball like that. (Former Steelers quarterback Mark Malone once told me that Bradshaw could throw a football 100 yards.)

"I was always pretty good at throwing a football," I said to Bradshaw. "I could throw a 55-yard spiral in my prime, but when I try to throw a pass with my finger on the end, it goes end over end like a punt."

I was expecting a detailed, technical explanation for why gripping the ball like a dart allowed him to throw so well, but this is what I got:

"You don't have the 'T.' "

I said, "What do you mean?"

Again, "You don't have the 'T.' "

I figure I'll bite. "What's the 'T' "?

"The talent. The talent." (With a strong emphasis on the "T.")

Obviously, Bradshaw was right.

CHAPTER 2

SHORT STOP

ME AND MR. McFEELY

I found out early on that when you're trying to sell a book, it's a good idea to go to a lot of book signings. In December of 2010, I was out signing copies of "Just Watch the Game" just about every weeknight and all day on weekends.

I was pleasantly surprised by the turnout and it was a reflection of the popularity of the book. I was actually stunned by how many copies I sold. I also have to admit that I was always a little worried about running into an offended or disgruntled reader.

Maybe a family member of someone I wrote about.

My biggest worry was that I would run into someone from Mister Rogers' family. He was a Pittsburgh icon and there's a chapter in the book called "Mister Rogers or the Three Stooges?"

Here's an excerpt:

Let's say you're in the market for a babysitter for your 5-year-old son and your next-door neighbor says, "I have the perfect guy for you."

I don't know about you, but my first response would be, "Guy?"

And your neighbor says, "Yeah, trust me. He's just a guy who really loves little kids. He runs a daycare center. Your son will love him."

You decide to pay Mister Rogers a visit and you're sitting in his living room when he comes in and says, "Hello, neighbor," takes off his baby-blue cardigan sweater, sits down, takes off his shoes and puts on a pair of sneakers that no self-respecting man would be caught dead in and pulls out a bunch of puppets. It becomes obvious to you right away that this guy really, really enjoys playing with puppets. It also becomes obvious to you that this guy is a major-league sissy.

Would you really want your kid to hang around with this guy for more than five minutes?

Fortunately for me, all my signings were peaceful and I never had to call security. But there was one major uncomfortable moment.

It was a Saturday afternoon signing at Borders in the Pittsburgh Mills Mall.

When I walked into the Borders, the manager welcomed me and told me how thrilled she was to have me, but she also said that she hoped that I wouldn't mind sharing a signing table with another local author.

I said I had no problem with that and then she said, "That's great, I'm sure you'll have fun. It's Mr. McFeely from 'Mister Rogers' Neighborhood.'"

"Oh, great," I said.

On the way to the back of the store I was trying to think of what I could come up with as an excuse to bail on the book signing. Then I started wondering if Mr. McFeely had read the book and I was trying to imagine what it would be like sitting next to a guy who wanted to punch me in the mouth for four hours.

Mr. McFeely was in full deliveryman uniform when we met and he couldn't have been nicer. It was obvious that he hadn't read my book.

We were seated at a long table and he was to my left.

I had several copies of "Just Watch the Game" stacked in front of me and he had pictures of himself and some pamphlets and some other items related to the "Mister Rogers' Neighborhood" TV show.

I was shocked by the number of people who stopped by to see him. It was mostly young mothers who had watched him when they were kids, and they wanted their kids to have their pictures taken with him.

Every time he posed for a picture, Mr. McFeeley would stand up, cock his head, hold up his hand and deliver his signature line, "Speedy delivery." He had a lot more traffic than I did.

I didn't mind because I was selling books for $20 and he was mostly giving away free autographed pictures or posing with the kiddies. I signed over 100 books that day.

We got along great and had an ongoing conversation during the breaks in the action, but I kept hoping that he wouldn't pick up a copy of my book. I had done my best to place the books so that he wouldn't see the excerpt on the back cover that read:

"ON MISTER ROGERS AS A ROLE MODEL:
"Given a choice, I always preferred the Three Stooges."

Mr. McFeely was busy enough that he never had a chance to pick up a copy of "Just Watch the Game," but I was almost busted when a customer who was looking through my book about 20 feet away yelled to me, "Hey, Stag, how can you be sittin' next to that guy when you wrote this?"

Mr. McFeely didn't hear him because he was busy posing for a picture.

I gave him the "Ssshhh" sign and a face that was pleading with him to give me a break and the guy laughed and went back to reading my book.

A couple of hours into the signing session, Mr. McFeely says, "By the way, before we go, I want to get you to sign a couple copies of your book for my two sons."

Uh, oh.

"Sure," I said, and then spent the next hour or so hoping that he would forget and that I could slink out of the store like the coward that I am.

Finally, some time in hour three, during a lull, Mr. McFeely says, "Hey, why don't you sign those books now."

I said "OK" and grabbed a book, opened it up and asked him his son's name.

I started to sign it and then I said, "You know what, before I sign this, I think I should show you something."

I turned the book over and showed him the line that read, "Given a choice, I always preferred the Three Stooges."

Mr. McFeely read it while I braced myself for the indignant outburst if not the punch in the mouth.

Mister Rogers would have been proud of Mr. McFeely's response:

"Oh, that's nothing. You should hear what Howard Stern says about us."

I hope his sons enjoyed the book.

CHAPTER 3

BIRDLAND

I'm guessing I was 10 or 11 years old.

I'm in the car with my dad, riding shotgun as we drive along North Wren Drive in Scott Township. (It's going to become clear very soon why this chapter is called Birdland, stick with me.) It's dark, probably around eight o'clock at night and it's drizzling.

I notice that we're slowing down as we approach the figure of a man up ahead. My dad tells me to roll down my window and he yells, "Hey, Fritzie, you want a ride?"

Fritzie obviously did because the next thing I knew I was in the back seat and he was riding shotgun. I remember thinking that it was kind of strange for my dad to stop and offer someone a ride but I didn't pay much attention to their conversation.

After three or four minutes, we pulled up in front of Fritzie's house on Cardinal Drive. Fritzie said his thank yous, reached back and patted me on the head, told me that he enjoyed meeting me and headed for his front door.

As we're pulling away, my dad says, "You know who that was?"

I said, "Some guy named Fritzie?"

He said, "That was Fritzie Zivic, the former welterweight champ." To which I replied, "Oh, you mean the Welterweight Champion of Pittsburgh." The old man was starting to lose his patience.

"No. The former Welterweight Champion of the World."

Keep in mind that this was the late '50s, when boxing really mattered and kids like me, who regularly watched the Friday night fights on NBC's "Gillette Cavalcade of Sports," knew who the champions of the various divisions were.

I was very much aware of guys like Floyd Patterson, Ingemar Johanssen, Carmen Basilio, Gene Fulmer, Jake LaMotta and Sugar Ray Robinson. They were champions of the world.

By the time we drove the two or three minutes to our house on Raven Drive, I had probably asked my dad if it was really true that this guy was a former Welterweight Champion of the World enough times that he wished he hadn't given Fritzie the ride.

If it had been 2011, I would have gone directly to my computer and Googled "Fritzie Zivic," but this was 1958 or 1959, so I went directly to my paperback version of the World Almanac.

I used to love looking through that book. It had everything from all the World Series and batting title winners to the names of every vice president.

When I got to the section on boxing champions and saw Fritzie Zivic next to 1940 under "Welterweight Champions," I was in shock.

The fact that I had just ridden in a car with someone whose name was in the World Almanac was even more unbelievable to me than the fact that I had ridden in the same car with a former Welterweight Champion of the World.

And there were no initials after Fritzie's name. No WBA or WBC. There was one Welterweight Champion of the World in 1940 and he was now living on Cardinal Drive, one street behind me and about 10 houses up.

It was my first brush with fame.

After a while, I realized that I had actually seen Fritzie many times but had never paid much attention to him as he walked his dog in the neighborhood. I just thought he was a guy walking his dog.

After finding out who he was, I thought it was very cool that his dog — a boxer, of course — was named "Champ."

Since my dad had given him that ride, I thought I had a lifetime license to talk to Fritzie whenever I saw him and Champ walking through the neighborhood and he always acted happy to see me.

I always tried not to look directly at his nose when I was talking to him, but that was almost impossible because he had more nose than face. A hundred and twenty-nine pro fights will get you punched in the nose a lot.

Fritzie was also living proof that 129 fights will get you a couple of world-class cauliflower ears. He won 100 of those fights with 50 knockouts and was only knocked out four times. Fritzie took a lot of punches.

I can remember bragging to my Uncle Red, on one of our trips to his home in Canada, that I lived one street away from a former Welterweight Champion of the World. I was a little disappointed and pissed off when Uncle Red said, "Fritzie Zivic was the dirtiest fighter I ever saw. He used to stand on guys' toes and then stick his thumb in their eye."

Fritzie Zivic (right) with Bennie Samuels and the great Sugar Ray Robinson (left) in the early '50s. This was the only picture hanging in Bennie's Saloon on 1st Avenue in downtown Pittsburgh. (photo courtesy Stu Samuels)

Uncle Red knew his boxing.

Fritzie was a dirty fighter and made no apologies. In fact, after he retired, he used to complain that there weren't enough good, dirty fighters around anymore.

He was also a busy fighter.

How busy? In 1936 he fought 18 times.

Sugar Ray Leonard fought 40 times in his career.

In the '30s and '40s, Pittsburgh was making a good case for being the boxing capital of the world and that was a time when being a boxer was a much bigger deal than being a pro football player. I had shared a ride with a guy who was a big, big deal in Pittsburgh at one time.

Imagine what it must have been like in Pittsburgh on December 28, 1936 at the Duquesne Gardens. Fritzie Zivic, from Lawrenceville, fighting Billy Conn of Greenfield, the future light-heavyweight champion who should have beaten Joe Louis.

Conn won on a controversial split decision.

Nobody gave Fritzie a chance when he fought one of the greatest fighters of all time, Henry Armstrong, for the welterweight title on October 4, 1940 at Madison Square Garden. It was one of the dirtiest, nastiest fights in boxing history in front of what is still the biggest crowd ever for a boxing match at MSG — 23,190. Fritzie made it into the World Almanac on a unanimous decision.

So, Fritzie was Birdland's most famous citizen. But, as you'll see, he wasn't the only famous citizen.

You've probably noticed that the streets in my neighborhood were named after birds. The official name for the housing plan, which was built in the mid-1950s and included the first homes built by a young Pittsburgh guy named Ed Ryan, was and still is St. Clair Heights, but everybody knows it as Birdland. I grew up on Raven, which sits below Cardinal and above Grouse. Blue Jay and Meadowlark are above Cardinal.

What a great neighborhood to grow up in. Virtually every house on every street was filled with kids. I knew several families with double-digit kids. The streets were crawling with them. It was Baby Boomers in full boom – and with virtually no parental oversight.

The Raven-Cardinal baseball game became an annual event. The kids organized it. No parents. No umpires. No uniforms. No snacks. We stood up and pedaled our bikes as fast as we could down the huge hills. No helmets.

For some reason, Birdland attracted famous people — mostly sports figures.

Up on Cardinal, just down the street from Fritzie Zivic, was Tom Bender, who shared the Steelers radio play-by-play duties with Joe Tucker and also called Penn State football games and worked as a sportscaster on KDKA -TV. (He was one of my paper-route customers.) Bender also was host of Pittsburgh's first radio sports talk show on WTAE. He did it for one year and was replaced in 1973 by some guy named Myron Cope.

Ed Conway, the man who preceded Bill Hillgrove as the radio voice of Pitt football and basketball and worked for several years as the sports director at WTAE-TV, also lived on Cardinal, about 10 houses away from Tom Bender.

Richie Zisk, a great hitter for the Pirates in the early-to-mid-1970s, spent a few years living on Blue Jay Drive, the street above Cardinal. Ron Schock, the captain of the Penguins during that same period, also lived on Blue Jay, just down the street from Richie Zisk.

When the Penguins came to town in 1967, their first general manager, Jack Riley, moved into a house on Grouse Drive, the street just below Raven. As I write this, he is 91 years old, still lives in the same house and still goes to every Penguins game.

Riley moved in next door to my brother Paul's friend, Don Rectenwald, and Riley was always giving out free tickets to the neighborhood kids. Those tickets eventually led to Paul becoming the TV voice of the Penguins.

Ron Jaye, who spent over 30 years on Pittsburgh radio and TV and hosted Pittsburgh's first TV talk show, lived for many years on Blue Jay.

Pittsburgh got its first and only (thank God) major professional soccer team in 1967. They were called the Phantoms and the star player was a guy named Co Prins. He came here from Holland and could have lived anywhere but he chose to live between the Zivics and the Benders on Cardinal Drive. The Phantoms lasted one year, but, 14 years later, Co Prins had a role in Sylvester Stallone's World War II soccer movie, "Victory."

Co wasn't the only star of stage and/or screen to live on Cardinal Drive. In 1963, a kid named Kurt Yagjian moved in a few houses away from the Zivics. He was an opera star who played the title role in NBC's telecast of "Amahl and the Night Visitors" that used to be aired during Christmas and Easter. You can also catch Kurt on DVD in the 1973 production of "Jesus Christ Superstar." I'm pretty sure he played Jesus.

I'm also pretty sure that, if the real Jesus had come back to Earth in the early to mid- '60s, He would have moved into Birdland — probably a few doors down from the Zivics on Cardinal — and he would have been on my paper route.

For a while in the mid-1960s, the biggest story in Pittsburgh was "The Commuter Bandit." He was driving the cops crazy by robbing banks in the city and then escaping by bus to the suburbs. The cops were pretty sure he was making his getaways on a bus, but they couldn't figure out which one.

On May 17, 1967 "The Commuter Bandit" robbed the Bloomfield branch of Pittsburgh National Bank. For the second time. The cops said it was his 16th bank robbery and he had stolen a total of more than $200,000 (about $1.3 million in 2011 dollars.)

A little over a month later, on June 23, William Zieler was arrested and charged with being "The Commuter Bandit." The Zeilers lived on Blue Jay Drive, about 200 yards away from the Zivics, the Benders and the Prinses.

Meanwhile, one street away from the Zeilers there was a little kid in the second or third grade who probably was running the best Kool-Aid stand in Birdland and was on his way to making his first billion. Mark Cuban lived on Meadowlark.

WHILE WE'RE ON THE SUBJECT

Fritzie Zivic punched one of my best friends in the nose.

Mike Morasca, who lived on Blue Jay, was/is as tough as anybody I have ever met and that includes all the professional athletes. When he was 11 or 12, he decided to check out the kids' boxing camp that Fritzie had decided to run out of his house. There was a ring set up in the basement and kids were given free boxing lessons by a former Welterweight Champion of the World whose name could be found in the World Almanac.

Mike got into the ring for a little sparring and instruction. He remembers what happened like it was yesterday:

"I must have landed a lucky punch and Fritzie's reflexes kicked in. *Thwap*. The next thing I knew I was actually seeing stars and I could feel the blood running from my nose, which I knew was broken."

"Fritzie was terrified. He packed some cotton in my nostrils and walked me home." (A four or five minute walk.)

"When he saw my dad, he started apologizing all over the place and my dad said, 'Fritzie, don't worry about it. It'll toughen him up.' "

Mike's not sure but he thinks his dad straightened his nose right after Fritzie left. There was no trip to the hospital.

Let's pause and imagine this happening in 2011: Sugar Ray Leonard punches an 11-year-old kid and breaks his nose. Someone would have been recording it on a cell phone and it would have been up on YouTube in five minutes and received several million hits. The video would have been all over "SportsCenter" and every TV news outlet in the world. There would be talk of a multi-million dollar lawsuit and Sugar Ray would be called a child abuser.

Back then, it was no big deal. It probably did toughen Mike up. And Mike wanted me to make sure that you knew the most important part of the story.

He didn't go down.

Remember, I said Mike was tough? He passed that on to his only child, Jenna. She was the winner of "Survivor: The Amazon" on CBS in 2003.

WHILE WE'RE STILL ON THE SUBJECT

Lots of kids in Birdland learned about the power of the media because of my brother Bill and Tom Bender's decision to live on Cardinal Drive.

One summer day when I was 10 or 11, a few of us were begging Ken Isles, who lived two doors down, to let us borrow his tennis ball for a game of Home Run Derby that we were going to play up on Cardinal. Ken's mother had a strict policy about not letting kids play with Ken's toys unless Ken was involved, but Ken figured he'd take a chance and let us have the ball, even though he wasn't going to be involved in the game.

Of course, about five minutes later, as were walking up on Cardinal, somebody missed a throw and the ball went down the storm sewer.

We knew Ken would get in trouble if we came back without his ball, so a couple of the bigger kids volunteered my brother Bill to go down after it.

If it had been a manhole, it wouldn't have been a problem. We climbed in and out of those all the time. All we needed was a pick axe. But this was a grate set against the curb. Bill had to slither through the top and drop down into the sewer. He found the ball easily and flipped it topside. Then he realized he couldn't get out.

My big brother was caught in a sewer.

It didn't take long for the word to spread. Remember, the neighborhood was crawling with kids and they weren't inside playing video games. They were playing outside. Pretty soon, there were 70 to 100 kids gathered around the sewer on Cardinal Drive with my 11- or 12-year-old brother looking up at them helplessly from below the grate.

Some of us began to think that he was never going to get out and would be washed away with the next big rain. My brother's plight created enough of a spectacle that Mrs. Bender, whose house was across the street, thought it was worth a call to KDKA radio.

Eventually someone, maybe Mrs. Bender, also called the local volunteer fire department. The fire truck and the KDKA radio news car arrived at the sewer at about the same time.

It took less than 10 seconds for a fireman with an ax to chop away the asphalt that prevented the grate from being removed and spring my brother. When Bill climbed out, he was greeted by Mike Levine of KDKA.

Bill made the KDKA Radio news that night. I can still see Levine sitting in our dining room, calling in his story. The only thing I can remember was the beginning of his report, which began with, "Little Billy Steigerwald ...."

Who knew that, 50 years later, I would have my own talk show on KDKA in Mike Levine's old time slot. I don't know if Ken Isles' mother ever found out how close he came to losing his tennis ball that exciting afternoon in Birdland.

CHAPTER 4

SHORT STOP

BEST NICKNAME EVER

I'm not going to use Eddie's real last name because I don't want to embarrass him or his family, so let's call him Eddie Meadows.

Eddie was a big, slightly overweight but not obese, clumsy kid, who was a couple of years older than I.

He became legendary when, at age 14, he reported to South Hills Catholic High School as a freshman and, on the first day of gym class, revealed that he was incapable of doing a jumping jack.

From that day on he was known as "Phys Ed."

I don't know who came up with the nickname, but it was probably another 14-year-old kid and I think that shows amazing creativity and a great sense of humor for a kid that age.

Eddie eventually was called "Fizzer" for short and never seemed to be too crazy about either nickname.

I'm wondering, are kids required to do jumping jacks anymore, or are they considered dangerous because of the potential harm to their self-esteem?

CHAPTER 5

A WEEK IN CYBER HELL

'm old.

Turned 63 just before this book went to print.

I'm not as old as 63-year-old guys were when I was a kid, though.

When I was a kid, all 63-year-old guys looked like Dwight D. Eisenhower.

Back then, a 63-year-old guy never wore a pair of Bermuda shorts, much less a pair of workout shorts, and may or may not have owned a pair of "sneakers."

In the '50s, guys in their sixties always wore dress pants pulled up well above the navel by suspenders. They wore only old man shoes and they wore those black see-through socks with garter belts and they had really white legs even in summer.

They smoked cigars right down to the end and when it wasn't lit, they would chew on it.

For days.

If they had owned a Ford in 1943, they owned one in 1963 and if they made it that far, they'd own one in 1973.

A Chevy guy was a Chevy guy.

Sixty-three-year old guys didn't ride motorcycles and they didn't blast loud music in their cars.

Mr. Lupenac next door was 63 and he wore suspenders and walked a little hunched over. I don't think anybody ever saw him jogging and I know he didn't own a bike.

So 2011's 63 is 1960's 43 or, at the very least, 53.

But one of the curses that comes with age is the ability to compare. I know lots of things were better when I was younger but people who weren't alive when I was alive don't want to hear it. Just as I wasn't all that interested in hearing a 63-year-old guy constantly telling me how wonderful things were in the 1920s.

So, because I'm old, there are things today that I just either don't understand or refuse to accept.

Like grown men wearing replica team jerseys to games.

Sorry, I just don't get a 30-something guy wearing a Sidney Crosby 87 jersey to a Penguins game or, for that matter, anywhere. And I sure as hell can't understand a 50- or 60-something guy wearing one.

I've tried to picture my dad, who was a huge sports fan, sitting next to me at Forbes Field in 1960, when he was 40, wearing a Roberto Clemente jersey.

When people have heard me say that, they have come back with the argument that replica jerseys for adults weren't available back then.

No kidding.

You know why? Because no adult would have been caught dead in one.

I think grown-ups look ridiculous sitting next to their kids wearing identical jerseys. Call me crazy, but I always thought that kids shouldn't be treated as equals and that adults were supposed to be, you know, mature.

I think it's kind of girly for a guy to be wearing another man's jersey. It reminds me of a high school girl wearing her boyfriend's letter jacket.

Do girls still do that?

Are there still letter jackets?

Now, it doesn't make me right and you wrong if you choose to wear one and please, if you happen to run into me at a Penguins game and you're wearing your Brooks Orpik jersey, understand that the fact that I think it's girly doesn't mean that I think I can beat you up.

Remember, I'm old.

You're supposed to feel sorry for me or at least have mercy on me.

• • •

This is the second book that I've written with the theme "Just Watch the Game" running through it and if you read the first book and came back for more, you know that, for me, it's always been about the game and I'm bothered by the fact that watching the game seems to be becoming less and less important to people who show up at stadiums or watch sports on TV.

It seems to have become all about the tailgating, fantasy sports (another thing I don't get and refuse to accept), drinking, jersey wearing and trying to show the person sitting next to you that you're the biggest fan in the building.

Violence has also become more of a problem and I've felt for a while that the jerseys and the attitude that goes with wearing them have been a major reason for it.

So in April of 2011, a few days after a Giants fan wearing a replica jersey to the Dodgers' home opener had been beaten into an induced coma by two animals wearing Dodger blue outside of Dodgers Stadium, I wrote this in my Sunday column, which was carried by three local newspapers:

Maybe it's time for sports fans to grow up.

As I'm writing this, Bryan Stow, a 42-year-old paramedic with two kids from Sacramento, is lying comatose in a Los Angeles hospital with a fractured skull and serious brain injuries.

Part of his skull had to be removed in order to allow for the swelling of his brain.

Stow went to the Los Angeles Dodgers' home opener on April 1st wearing a San Francisco Giants jersey. That was obviously too much for two 20-something guys wearing Dodger blue to handle. Witnesses say that, after the game, they came up on Stow from behind in the parking lot, knocked him down and kicked him as they spewed expletives about the San Francisco Giants.

It's probably safe to say that the two "Dodgers" were high on something or things, but somewhere in their sick, juvenile minds they probably also thought that they were doing their duty as Dodger fans.

They were protecting Dodger turf.

Just before he was beaten within an inch of his life, Stow texted some friends and said that he was "scared inside the stadium." Maybe somebody can ask Stow, if he ever comes out of his coma, why he thought it was a good idea to wear Giants gear to a Dodgers' home opener when there was a history of out-of-control drunkenness and arrests at that event going back several years.

Remember when it was the kids who were wearing the team jerseys to games? It was a common sight to see an adult male coming through the turnstile dressed as a regular human being with a kid dressed in a "real" jersey holding his hand.

Cute.

Are the 42 year olds who find it necessary to wear their replica jerseys to a road game those kids who are now fathers who haven't grown up?

Are there really 40-something men who think that wearing the jersey makes them part of the team? It was cute when a 10-year-old kid got that feeling by showing up at Three Rivers Stadium in a Pirates jersey, but when did little boys stop growing out of that?

Here's tip for you if you actually think that wearing your team's jersey makes you a part of the team:

It doesn't.

The team is those guys down on the field, ice or court who are, you know, actually playing the games. They like the noise that you make as a group and they love playing in front of you, but, if you're an adult and you approach them in a replica game jersey with their name on it and your face is painted, you scare them.

If you don't put that jersey on in the locker room with them and have your own name on your jersey, you're not one of them.

Let's review: If you're sitting in the stands, you're a spectator —a fan. If you're down on he field, you're part of the team.

Obviously, not every fan who wears his team's jersey to a game is looking for someone from "the enemy" to beat up, but maybe somebody should do a psychological study to find out if all of those game jerseys have contributed to the new mob mentality that seems to exist in the stands these days.

(There's an outside chance that alcohol plays a role, but, apparently, the teams have ruled that out and continue to sell nine dollar beers.)

If you're one of two or three guys wearing Steelers jerseys sitting in the middle of the Dog Pound in Cleveland, guess what, the Steelers players can't see you and even if they could, they're not really getting a lot of inspiration from you.

And, if you're set upon by a bunch of drunken adults wearing dog costumes, you probably shouldn't expect any help from the guys on the field who are wearing the jerseys that look just like yours.

So, why not just go to the Browns game in Cleveland dressed as a regular human being? When did it become necessary to wear a uniform to the game?

• • •

Talk about the shit hitting the fan.

I was eating dinner in a restaurant with my family when I got a call from former WPXI-TV sports anchor John Fedko. He said, "You have to turn on The Fan. You're getting killed on there. Who's Chris Muller?"

Muller was/is the 10-2 p.m. host at 93.7 The Fan in Pittsburgh and he was filling in on the 6-10 shift. He was on the air calling me a hack and trashing me for having spat in the face of the fans who helped me have a long career in Pittsburgh TV and radio. He, of course, was referring to my comments about adults wearing jerseys. He went on to say that I had either blamed Brian Stow (whose name, unfortunately, I had printed incorrectly as Snow) for getting beat up or said that he deserved it.

Maybe both.

I called the show and we had a heated discussion, during which Muller said that what I had written was the same as blaming a provocatively dressed woman for being raped. It was the first time I would hear ridiculous analogies being made about what I said but it sure wouldn't be the last.

I don't know who was the first to pick up the column and send it out on the Internet, but by later that night it had gone viral.

It's important to point out that the column had appeared in the three local papers two days earlier and had been available on the websites of the Washington (Pa.) Observer-Reporter, the Indiana (Pa.) Gazette and the Valley News Dispatch for three days and received virtually no negative feedback.

By Wednesday afternoon I was being picked up by a limo and taken to a satellite-feed studio downtown for an appearance on the nationally syndicated TV show "Inside Edition." My feeling that I was making a mistake was confirmed by the 90-second hatchet job that the show's producers did on me.

From coast-to-coast I was being called "The Most Hated Man in America."

Bloggers, who accused me of writing the story for the sole purpose of increasing traffic to my website, used my story to increase traffic to their websites. It didn't matter that I wrote the piece for the three newspapers that weren't linked to my site and that it generated zero hits until it went viral.

All over North America people were seeing headlines that went something like this:

"Jerk in Pennsylvania says Giants Fan Deserved It"

" Pennsylvania Columnist Says Stow had it Coming"

"Stow Was Asking For It Says Pa. Columnist."

My wife Jeani was more upset about the reaction than I was.

What bothered me most was that my nine-year-old grandson had been in the car and had heard his Pop being referred to as the most hated man in America.

When it comes to handling criticism, you probably don't know anybody who has thicker skin than mine. That doesn't mean that I accept it without defending myself.

I read the column a hundred times and I knew that I never said or insinuated that Brian Stow deserved what happened to him.

I knew that the hysteria had reached the point of no return when I read a sports blogger for the Washington Times who wrote that I said it was *permissible* for fans to beat a visiting fan within an inch of his life if he's wearing the wrong jersey.

I refused to accept what bloggers and columnists were saying that I said.

I went on radio in Toronto, Seattle and Philadelphia and refused to back down.

On Philadelphia's KYW Radio, the host, Dom Giordano, also told me that I said that Bryan Stow deserved it. I said that I couldn't believe that a guy as successful and as smart as he is could make the jump from questioning Stow's judgment — which I was happy to admit that I had done — to saying that he deserved it.

Then he said, "John, you're saying that a Giants fan can't go to a Dodgers' game wearing his Giants jersey without taking a beating."

That really pissed me off.

I said very loudly, "No, Don. I'm not saying that at all, but you know who did say it? The two animals who beat Bryan Stow within an inch of his life."

The conversation ended shortly after that.

I spent several hours Wednesday and Thursday night responding to people on my website who were attacking me and telling me that I deserved to die. It's my website and I'm the only person who decides whether the responses are posted and I posted all but the ridiculously vulgar ones.

It wasn't until Thursday of my week in Internet Hell that I called Dale Lolley, a long time sports writer for the Washington Observer-Reporter, and asked him if this column that had created hysteria around the world had generated any more response than usual after it appeared Sunday.

He said, absolutely not. He hadn't received one phone call or angry email. I checked with the other two papers and they said the same thing.

It was then that I realized what had happened.

I wrote a column for three small newspapers aimed at the people who have been reading my columns for 25 years. I wasn't concerned about being insensitive to the Stow family because I never dreamed that they would read the column. Out-of-control, immature fans was a subject that I had written about many times before and I assumed that my audience would know exactly what I meant.

I also assumed that people who had been reading my column for 25 years would know that if I wanted to say that Bryan Stow deserved what he got, here's how I would have written it:

"Bryan Stow deserved what he got."

During the week I received several encouraging emails from my friends in the local media telling me that they knew exactly what I was saying and to hang in there.

My column in the local papers was not seen as all that controversial and it had been taken in the context and spirit that it had been written.

The shit hit the fan when the shit hit the fan.

All over the English-speaking world, people were being directed to my column by headlines like the ones I listed above. They came to it with the preconceived notion that I had said that Bryan Stow deserved to be beaten to within an inch of his life.

What ended up pissing me off the most were the self-righteous bloggers who were more than happy to increase traffic to their sites by attacking me for shamelessly trying to increase traffic to my site. By making sure that they demonstrated their self-righteousness, they also made sure that the Stow family saw the insensitivity that offended them so much.

If the bloggers don't pick it up, the Stow family in San Francisco never sees it. Their concern for the family didn't quite override their own desire to create traffic for their sites.

As time has gone by, I've become much more defiant.

I'm even more convinced that I never said or even insinuated that Bryan Stow deserved or asked for what he got.

A few days after things had calmed down, I came across an interview that one of Stow's friends had done with ESPN Radio Los Angeles. He said that he and Bryan knew right away when they got to the stadium that they weren't welcome. He went on to say that all during the game he and his friends, including Stow, had "Popcorn, wrappers and hot dogs" thrown at them and he said, "But we expected that."

Sorry, but even though, tragically, as this book went to print, Stow was still hospitalized in serious condition, I have to question the judgment of a group of 40-something men who make the decision to put on a shirt that they know will result in them at least having hot dogs thrown at them. Especially when they had to be aware of the problem with fan violence at Dodgers Stadium.

Lots of people got lots of laughs at my expense when I suggested that the relatively new trend of adults wearing replica game jerseys to games was a sign that things had gotten out of hand and could be blamed for much of the violence among fans.

They should go into fits of uncontrollable laughter when they read what Doctor Irving Goldaber said to Sports Illustrated way back in 1983. Goldaber, who died several years ago, was a sociologist and the director of the Center for Study of Crowd and Spectator Behavior in Miami.

He spent a good deal of his life studying crowds and was, for many years, the country's foremost and most sought-after authority on the subject. He advised NFL and Major League Baseball teams and the International Association of Chiefs of Police.

Other than that, he has no credibility on the subject of what can lead to violence at sports events.

Here's what Sports Illustrated wrote about him in a major story about fan violence that appeared in their Jan. 31, 1983, issue.

During the 1950s and 1960s, Goldaber, who says, "Human conflict was always my field," instructed law enforcement groups in dealing with street disturbances, protestors, terrorists and hostage takers. In the mid-'70s, he says, he detected the emergence of a new form of violence in this country. He terms it "violence for vicarious power" and finds it's most openly manifested in sporting crowds.

Specifically, he says, "More and more people aren't making it. You work hard, you exist, but you haven't got much to show for it. There are increasing numbers of people who are deeply frustrated because they feel they have very little power over their lives. They come to sporting events to experience, vicariously, a sense of power.

"In a stadium, the power trippers are even more vulnerable to ordinary crowd stimuli and irritations than more traditional fans. They respond to the violence on the field. They respond to the hype and the hoopla of the event, to the beer, cheerleaders, scoreboards and bands. When you have a crowd that is anticipating a physical experience, it will have a physical experience."

Now for the best part:

Goldaber believes that several characteristics distinguish the vicarious power seekers. (See if you recognize any of these people.) *They're very prone* (Are you ready?) *to over-identify with a team or individuals. "They're dressed in the numbers and letters and the names and the colors with the jackets, the sweaters, the scarves and the pennants," he says. "They're part of the team and they're in the game....*

"Because they over-identify and think they're in the game, they feel they have a right to affect the outcome of the game. In the old ways by cheering and booing, but also with violent forms of threatening and intimidating action.

"Because winning, being number one, is everything, they're likely to be very ferocious if they — their team — are thwarted and they vent their frustrations physically against players, officials or other spectators. That's the rub of the problem."

I rest my case.
Just Watch the Game.

CHAPTER 6

PINCH HITTING FOR YOGI

It was probably some time in December of 1983 when Channel 4 news director Joe Rovitto came to me with the idea.

He wanted me to try out for the Pirates.

I was 35 at the time and wasn't all that optimistic about my chances of making the club, but he was the boss, so I listened.

His idea was for me to go to spring training and actually train with the Pirates. Put on a uniform, take batting practice and *pretend* that I was trying out.

TV news directors and producers have a tendency to come up with ideas that sound really good but have no chance of ever showing up on anybody's television and at first that's what I thought I was dealing with. I figured I would run it by the Pirates and they would shoot me down immediately.

They loved the idea.

That surprised me and it also worried me because I wondered if maybe the Pirates were looking at it as a way to expose a local TV sports guy as an un-athletic geek who should never critique or question a Major League Baseball player again.

It turned out that they just thought it was a good idea.

So, the boss and the Pirates were happy.

I, of course, was the 35-year-old guy who had to show up in the Pirates' spring-training locker room in Bradenton, Fla., put on a uniform and take the field with Major League Baseball players and not make a fool of myself.

The fact that I hadn't played baseball in about 25 years was a real boost for my confidence.

I had played my last organized baseball game for the Corsairs in the Scott Township Youth Baseball league in the summer of 1960. Grounded out to second in the last at bat of my mediocre career, if I'm not mistaken.

I had played lots of softball and I was a pretty good centerfielder and leadoff hitter for the always-dangerous "Channel 4 No Stars," WTAE's barnstorming team. I could still run and throw and was even known to make a crowd pleasing catch in the gap once in a while.

But that was *softball.*

You know, underhanded pitching, short base paths and compact outfields.

And the plan in Bradenton didn't end with me taking batting practice or going through a few drills.

I was going to play in an *intrasquad* game.

That meant live pitching, umpires, keeping score and people in the stands.

Uh oh.

I had about six weeks to get ready and I knew I had to face some live pitching, not an easy thing to do in Pittsburgh in January. Fortunately, the Pitt baseball team was working out at Fitzgerald Field House in preparation for its season that would be opening in Florida in a few weeks.

I talked a couple of their pitchers into throwing to me in the batting cage a couple of times a week.

Conditioning was also an issue. I was in pretty good shape for a 35-year-old sportscaster, but I didn't want to embarrass myself if I had to take part in any drills so I started going to the Mt. Lebanon High School field to run laps and 30-yard sprints (90 feet, get it?). I did as much stretching as I could and by the time I got to Bradenton in late February I was feeling pretty good about myself.

Until I walked into the locker room.

I had been in plenty of pro locker rooms, including after Super Bowls and World Series games, but I had never walked into one looking for my locker and my uniform.

The fact that there were several minor league players who had no idea who I was didn't help and self-conscious doesn't begin to describe the feeling I had when I started undressing in front of my locker while real Pirates like John Candelaria, Kent Tekulve, Bill Madlock and Doug Frobel, based on the looks I was getting, made it clear that they had no idea why I was there.

OK, I wasn't all that intimidated by Doug Frobel.

But this was the first day of camp for the regulars and you can imagine the kind of first-day-of-school feel that the room had.

Talk about feeling like the new kid. I felt like a new kid who showed up for the first day of school with one of those really big zits on the end of his nose.

The players, of course, made me feel comfortable right away by completely ignoring me.

I put my uniform on and hoped that I got the socks and stirrups right and walked out on to the practice field. I was actually looking forward to the first workout because I felt that my conditioning program, which included lots of stretching, had prepared me well enough to keep up.

Boy, was I wrong.

Going to Dunkin' Donuts every day would have been enough to prepare me for the "workout" that these Major League Baseball players did on their first day.

After all the players had assembled on the field, one of the coaches yelled, "OK, let's go," and everybody started jogging down the right field line toward home plate. I followed the group and we ran in front of home plate and up the leftfield line, coming to a stop in left-center field.

That was it. That was the beginning and the end of the running that the team did.

Not just that first day.

For the entire time that I was there.

After everybody arrived in left-center field it was time to stretch. I wasn't worried about that because a personal-trainer friend of mine had shown me some really good stretches, which I had been doing faithfully for several weeks.

I didn't need them, either.

The players stood with their sanitary socks held over their heads and "stretched" for a few minutes. The only thing missing were cigarettes.

I remember John Candelaria doing what was supposed to be a

toe-touching exercise by bending his waist no more than 10 percent of the way while he was talking to Bill Madlock, who was probably bending about eight percent.

So much for the grueling conditioning.

That was the routine every morning.

Once practice started I didn't do much other than shag flies during batting practice, which gave the cameraman, Tim Lohle, a chance to get some video of me on the field in my Pirates #4 uniform (Channel 4, get it?) with my name on the back. At the end of practice, strictly for the purposes of my story, a coach would pitch to me in the batting cage.

I don't remember much about the stories that I did those first few days, but I probably didn't rip their "conditioning" program because that would have made me look ungrateful.

After four of five days it was time to shoot the last installment of the series – the reason for our trip: my appearance in an actual intra-squad game.

I wish I could tell you that the players were interested in why I was in their dugout wearing a Pirates uniform but they couldn't have been more disinterested. It was as though they were going out of their way to let me know that I shouldn't be anywhere near their dugout and I sure as hell shouldn't be wearing their uniform.

They weren't nasty or even unfriendly. Just indifferent.

Imagine how comfortable that made me feel.

I could have used a little encouragement.

It was a good thing that my manager was one of the nicest guys in the history of sports, the late Chuck Tanner.

He couldn't have been nicer. Before the intra-squad game started he told me that I would be going into right field in the top of the 8th inning and that I would bat in the bottom of the 8th.

That gave me lots of time to sit in the dugout and ask myself what the hell I was doing there.

I took the field in the top of the eighth. Shagging balls in the outfield during batting practice had prepared me enough that I wasn't completely terrified to be standing where Roberto Clemente and Dave Parker had stood many times, but after playing so much softball, home plate looked like it was half a mile away.

In the time that I stood there, I went from thinking, "Please, don't hit it here" to "Go ahead, hit one in the gap, I'll run it down."

It was probably a good thing that it was a three-up, three-down inning and nothing came my way.

Now it was time for the culmination of our TV spectacular.

Me against Alfonso Pulido.

I can guarantee you that I am the only person on the planet who remembers that someone named Alfonso Pulido once pitched for the Pirates. He actually pitched a total of four innings for them — two in 1983 and two in 1984.

Pulido had been signed out of the Mexican League at the end of the 1983 season. He was one of many straws that the Pirates grasped for in the early '80s when they started to realize that they couldn't compete for free agents who could actually play.

Pulido was a star in the Mexican League and had won 20 games in 1983 for the Mexico City Reds. The Pirates were hoping that they had found a star. Maybe the next Fernando Valenzuela.

I was hoping he didn't hit me in the head with the first pitch.

Here's something you need to know: Alfonso didn't speak a word of English.

He had no idea who I was. As far as he was concerned, I was a guy in the Pirates' camp trying to make the team just like he was.

I was introduced by the P.A. announcer and went up to the plate, wired for sound with a wireless mic.

The first pitch was a fastball that I heard but didn't really see. Called strike one.

I tried for some levity and said to the catcher (I don't remember who it was), "Did he throw it yet?"

The catcher didn't laugh.

(Looking back on it, I'm glad that it was Pulido out there. Since he had no idea who I was or why I was there, I don't think he cut me any slack. He was really trying to get me out.)

I struck out swinging on the fourth pitch and headed back to the dugout feeling pretty good about myself for having had the guts to stand in there against a Major League pitcher and feeling like I had done a good job with the story.

The boss was going to love it.

When I got to the dugout, cameraman Lohle told me the one thing that a TV reporter never wants to hear when he just did a once-in-a-lifetime shot.

"You're not gonna believe this," he said, "but my battery died. I only got the first pitch." Tim is one of the best camera guys I ever worked with — very creative and as reliable and as hard working as they come — and he was beside himself. (He still works for Channel 4.)

I was never a guy to cry over spilled milk and I wasn't about to make a scene, but I knew we were in big trouble because everything we had done in Bradenton was leading up to the big moment when I batted in a Pirates intrasquad game. We couldn't end the piece with the one pitch that we had and it was the ninth inning of the last intrasquad game.

Tanner overheard Tim and me talking about what we were going to do and he said, "What's the matter?"

Most managers in that situation would have shrugged their shoulders and moved on — that's assuming that they would have allowed us to do the story at all — but not Chuck Tanner.

"Dale, come here," he yelled. Over comes Dale Berra, bat in hand. It's now the bottom of the ninth. Chuck nods towards me and says, "John's going to pinch hit for you here."

Berra laughs, thinking that Chuck's kidding. When he realizes that Chuck's serious, he starts protesting, "C'mon, Skip, I need my hacks."

It doesn't work.

I'm up next and I head for the on-deck circle, talking into the wireless mic as I go.

To this day, I'm still convinced that Pulido had no idea who I was and that he pitched to me the same as he would have pitched to any other hitter.

I took the first pitch for a ball. I think it was a fastball.

I swung at the next pitch and hit a shot right at the second baseman. OK, actually, it was a 17-hopper to the second baseman and was I thrown out easily.

Hey, I stood in there against a Major League Pitcher and made contact. That's all I wanted.

Those days in the batting cage at Fitzgerald Field house actually paid off by allowing me to get over any fear of standing in there against live pitching. The last hardball pitcher I had faced was 12 years old.

I wasn't quite as excited about my performance after looking at the tape. I saw that I was way too tentative and had swung off my back foot.

If I had been aggressive and stepped into it, I would have ripped it up the middle. Then I probably would have stolen second base and scored on a single to center. Head-first slide, of course. It might have been the beginning of a new career for me.

It was the beginning of the end of Pulido's career with the Pirates. He pitched one game for them in 1984 and was traded to the Yankees the following December for Steve Kemp.

The Pirates also threw in another player.

Dale Berra.

WHILE WE'RE ON THE SUBJECT

A few months later, I found out that the players were very much aware of my presence in the dugout. Kent Tekulve told me that every pitcher on the staff asked Chuck Tanner for a chance to pitch to me. I'm pretty sure it wasn't because they wanted to be able to tell their grandchildren about the time they pitched to a big-time local TV sportscaster.

CHAPTER 7

"THE COBRA"

The Pirates didn't have to wait long for a right fielder after Roberto Clemente died in 1972. Three seasons later they had one of the best players in baseball playing there.

Dave Parker was 24 when he started the 1975 season as the Pirates right fielder. He played in 148 games, hit .308 with 25 homeruns and 101 RBIs and had an arm that wasn't as good as Clemente's but was as good or better than any other right fielder in Major League Baseball.

Parker was big before steroids made almost every baseball player big — 6'5' and 230 pounds — and he had great speed. Parker was as intimidating as any player in baseball history. By 1978 — when he put up better numbers than Clemente ever had in a single season with 34 homeruns, 117 RBIs and .334 batting average — he was the best player in baseball and had a National League batting title and an MVP award to prove it.

In January of 1979 Parker became the first American professional athlete to earn an average of $1 million per year. That's right. The small-market, low-payroll, pathetic Pittsburgh Pirates were the first team to pay a player $1 million a year.

Of course, things were different then. Free agency had only been in effect for three years and the Pirates were still able to compete for the big-name players.

It wasn't long after Parker signed the million-dollar deal that Pirates fans started abusing him. On at least one occasion he had to leave the field during the game because fans were throwing batteries at him.

It was obvious that $1 million was the magic number for fans who were still getting used to players being paid what they could get on the open market instead of what the team that owned them forever wanted to pay them.

Most fans thought it was obscene for baseball players to be getting several hundred thousand dollars a year and three or four years earlier nobody could have imagined any player making a million bucks in one season.

The fact that Parker was black didn't help.

Parker had every right to be bitter about the way he was treated by the fans and he was. Not only had he put up some of the best offensive numbers in Pirates history, he never took a play off and would run full speed to first base even on a one-hop shot to the second baseman.

He ran the bases like a maniac and paid the price for it when he came out of a home-plate collision with Mets catcher John Stearns with a broken jaw and fractured cheek bone. That was on June 30, 1978. He came back on July 17 wearing a football face mask, went two for five with a triple and two runs batted in and went on to become the National League's Most Valuable Player.

Despite all of that, he was still being harassed by fans at Three Rivers Stadium. Parker was pissed off and confused. Actually, maybe he wasn't all that confused. He blamed it on the fact he was black and that white people couldn't handle a black man making the kind of money that he was making.

It was hard to argue with him.

One night during the 1979 season I did a commentary about Parker on WTAE's 11 o'clock news. I asked the viewers what there was *not* to like about Dave Parker. I rattled off his stats. I showed video of his home plate collision and I showed video of him running full speed on the bases wearing a football facemask. I probably threw in a couple of great throws from right field and I said, "And, as far as I know, he has never said anything bad about the Steelers."

The next day, Parker came up to me in the Pirates' dugout and said, "Hey, man, I saw what you said about me last night and I really appreciate it." Back then, Channel 4 replayed the 11 p.m. news at 2 a.m. and there was no ESPN "SportsCenter," so that's where the players went for their game highlights.

From that day on, I had a good relationship with Parker. That's good relationship as in "good player-microphone puke" relationship. It's not like we became good buddies and went on double dates.

Believe it or not, the commentary that I did would have been seen as controversial by a lot of people at the time. It had actually become fashionable to dislike Parker and I genuinely couldn't understand it.

Looking back on it, I still don't get it, but I have to say that racism and stupidity were the only explanations. And maybe the fact that he wasn't Roberto Clemente.

• • •

Parker's size and loud mouth created an image problem around the league, but a lot of that was also based on misunderstanding. Parker loved to get on his teammates and his verbal battles with Pirates second baseman Phil Garner are legendary. Out-of-town writers would see this gigantic man bellowing insults at everyone in sight and come away thinking Parker was a major-league asshole.

I saw a perfect example of that in 1981.

The Pirates had just brought Luis Tiant up from their AAA team in Hawaii. Tiant had already been in the big leagues for 17 years and was 40 years old. In 1981, 40 wasn't old.

It was ancient.

And nobody actually believed Tiant was really that young. But he had managed to hang on and after being just about un-hittable in Hawaii, he was given one more shot by the Pirates.

I happened to run into Tiant in the locker room a few hours before he was supposed to pitch his first game for the Pirates. He was the only player there except, unfortunately, Dave Parker.

I wandered in with my cameraman and headed toward Tiant and Parker went off. At the top of his lungs he yelled, "Come on. Leave the old man alone. This motherfucker is 57 years old and he's pitching for us tonight. Leave the motherfucker alone."

Just then, I noticed that an out-of-town writer was also in the locker room and I watched him slink out the door. I just laughed, and said, "OK,

Dave," and did my interview with Tiant.

I knew Parker was kidding. A couple of hours later as I was waiting for the press box elevator, the out-of-town writer who I had seen in the locker room came up to me and said, "Boy, that Parker is a real asshole, isn't he?"

Imagine how many times he told that story to his baseball-writer buddies over the years.

Despite the batting titles, MVP award and a World Series win in 1979, during that 1981 season Parker had as many detractors as fans in Pittsburgh and I still don't understand why.

There was a strike and a shortened season that year and that meant that we in the media were hurting for stories to do. I came up with the idea of paying a visit to Parker at his home in the North Hills for a long sit-down interview to talk about what he was doing during the strike and his relationship with Pittsburgh fans.

Parker liked the idea and I rounded up a crew.

Back then there were two-man crews — a cameraman and a guy who carried the videotape recorder. As the three of us were driving to Parker's house, the video man, Ben (no last names here), was going on and on about how he hated Dave Parker and how he told his young son that he should hate him, too. I tried to sell Ben on everything that Parker had done and he didn't want to hear it. He also said that he wasn't going to ask Parker to sign anything because he didn't want his son to have Parker's autograph.

When we got to Parker's house, he couldn't have been nicer. I kept glancing over at Ben to see how he was reacting to being in what had to be an awkward situation for him and he was just going about his business making sure that the tape was rolling.

I did the interview with Parker and then he took us into his game room and let us get some shots of his trophy case.

When we were finished, Parker says to Ben, "Do you have any kids." Ben tells Parker that he has a son and Parker says, "Do you want me to sign something for him?" Ben says he doesn't have anything for Parker to sign and Parker says, "Hold on, I'll be right back."

Parker went upstairs and came down with a brand new Major League quality glove, still wrapped in plastic, opens it up, asks Ben what his son's name is and signs the glove for him.

This was the guy Pittsburghers loved to hate.

Dave Parker made it two fewer haters that day.

Not long after that, Parker got fat and lazy and I became one of his biggest critics and was happy to see him leave. We found out during the Baseball Drug Trials of 1985 that Parker also was dabbling in cocaine the last few years that he was with the Pirates. It's probably safe to say that he ate and snorted his way out of the Baseball Hall of Fame, but, for most of his career, he may have been the most under-appreciated player in Pittsburgh sports history.

WHILE WE'RE ON THE SUBJECT

If you went to Pirates games in the late 1970s, you probably remember the big "Cobra" sign that hung from the upper deck in right field. The nickname that Bob Prince hung on Parker early in his career caught on with the public. Ask a Pirates fan where the nickname came from and he'll probably tell you that it had something to do with Parker's batting stance or his swing and that makes perfect sense.

But that's not where it came from.

"The Gunner" started calling Dave Parker "The Cobra" the first time he saw him coming out of the shower.

CHAPTER 8

BONDS OR CLEMENTE?

Seven hundred sixty-two to 240.

That's the difference in the number of home runs hit by Barry Bonds and Roberto Clemente. I don't think I have to tell you that Bonds has the 762.

That's a difference of 522 career home runs, but, you know what? I'm here to tell you that Bonds was not a better player than Clemente.

Look at the raw power numbers and it's no contest, but it's just not that simple.

Clemente played for 15½ seasons in the hardest ballpark in history for right-handed batters to hit home runs. Forbes Field opened in 1909 and closed in 1969. Do you know how many right-handed batters hit 30 or more home runs in a season for the Pirates?

Two.

And neither of them was named Ralph Kiner.

Frank Thomas (a Pittsburgh kid) did it twice. He hit 30 in 1953 and 35 in 1958. Dick Stuart was the only other hitter in 61½ seasons to hit more than 30. He had 35 in 1961.

Imagine only three right-handed batting Pirates hitting 30 or more home runs between now and 2070 at PNC Park.

OK, I forgot, we're talking about the Pirates.

Imagine a real Major League Baseball team playing in PNC Park and only having three right-handed batters hit more than 30 home runs in 61½ seasons.

Ralph Kiner hit 51, 40, 54, 47, 42 and 37 from 1947 to 1952, but he wasn't playing in the same Forbes Field that those other three guys played in. In 1947, the Pirates had talked Hank Greenberg, the great home run hitter for the Tigers, into extending his career by promising him that he wouldn't have to play in a ballpark that turned guys who swung for the fences into guys who made a lot of long outs.

The Pirates shrunk Forbes Field by running a cyclone fence from the left field line into centerfield and it became known as Greenberg Gardens. After Greenberg retired, the Pirates kept the low fence in place and it became known as Kiner's Korner. Before he put up those amazing numbers from 1947 through 1952, Kiner played one season in the real Forbes Field and hit 23 home runs.

That's why those raw power numbers for Clemente and Bonds can be so misleading.

When Clemente dug in at Forbes Field beginning in 1955, here's what he saw: Down the left field line it was 365 feet with a 25-foot scoreboard. Moving toward centerfield the 12-foot high brick outfield wall went to 406 and in almost straightaway center it reached 457. Moving toward right center, it was 436, then 375. Down the right field line it was 300 feet with a 27-foot high screen.

Kiner's Korner shortened the left field line to 335 and the 406 mark to 355. No wonder Kiner's home run totals were so ridiculous. And it's no wonder the home run totals were ridiculously low in the real Forbes Field. Kiner's 23 home runs led the National League in 1946, but only eight of them were hit at Forbes Field. In 1947, when he hit 51 with the help of Greenberg Gardens, 28 of them were hit at Forbes Field.

Bonds was a left-handed hitter, but how much do you think his home run totals would have been affected if he had played for 15½ seasons in a ballpark with dimensions on the right side of the field that were similar to what Clemente had to deal with from the left field line to right center?

Kiner's numbers are proof, just in case you needed it, of how much the size of the park can affect a home run hitter's totals.

Clemente hit 29 home runs in 1966, the fourth highest total at the real Forbes Field.

Let's do some math.

I don't think it would be outrageous to suggest that those ridiculous dimensions at Forbes Field swallowed up three Clemente drives a month that would have been home runs in any ballpark that Bonds played in from 1985 until 2007.

That's 18 home runs a year – again, not outrageous when you remember that Kiner doubled his home run totals when the fences were moved in. Over 15½ seasons, that's 279 more home runs for Clemente. Add that to the 240 that he hit in his career and we have a 500 home run man — 519 to be exact.

I don't think it's a stretch at all to suggest that Clemente would have hit as many career home runs as Ernie Banks did if he had played in Wrigley Field. Banks finished with 512. (Clemente still has the longest home run ever hit at Wrigley Field, by the way.)

It's also not a stretch to suggest that Banks would have had no more than 350 career home runs if he had played his entire career in Pittsburgh. (Use our three home runs per month theory and it comes out to 342 in a 19-year career.)

If you accept my premise that Forbes Field cost Clemente three home runs a month, then I'm sure that you'll be more than happy to agree that playing in a park with similar dimensions on the right side would have cost Bonds the same amount.

Bonds finished with 762 in 22 years. Three fewer home runs per month (18 a year times 22 years = 396) would have reduced that by more than half for a total of 366. Let's say it only would have cost Bonds two home runs per month for 22 years. That's 264 knocked off his total for a final number of 498.

I'm sorry, but when you consider that a right-handed batter was only able to hit 30 or more home runs at the real Forbes Field three times in nearly six decades, it's not a stretch to say that Bonds, facing the same dimensions on the right side of the field, would have had two long outs per month that would have been home runs in his three home ballparks in Pittsburgh and San Francisco.

Many of those impressive shots that Bonds hit to centerfield in Three Rivers Stadium and PacBell Park for home runs would have been long outs, doubles or triples at Forbes Field.

Of course, if their home run totals are adjusted Clemente's RBI totals would go up considerably and Bonds' would come down. To be fair,

Clemente's batting averages would not have been as high if not for all that space at Forbes Field.

Pitching was so dominant in the 1960s that, after the 1968 season, the pitcher's mound was lowered to make it easier for hitters. Clemente had the highest batting average in baseball for that decade, when starting pitchers with 2-something ERAs were commonplace. Bonds played in an era when teams were thrilled to have one starter with an ERA under 4.00.

Bonds has a huge edge in stolen bases, but Clemente played in an era when the stolen base was a lost art. There were fewer stolen bases from 1950 to 1970 than there were in any other 20-year period in Major League Baseball history. The only time there were more stolen bases than the '80s and '90s was during the dead-ball era from 1900 to 1920.

Clemente was every bit as fast as Bonds and would have been a prolific base stealer if called upon.

Do I really need to talk about defense?

Bonds, in his early years, was one of the best defensive left fielders I've ever seen, but come on, we're talking about Roberto Clemente here.

Oh yeah, and one other little item to consider.

Steroids.

They weren't around when Clemente played.

Everybody knows that Bonds was a steroid freak from 1999 on. He was hurt in 1999 and only played 105 games, but still managed to hit 34 home runs. (That's a 54 home-run pace.) From 2000 through 2004 he hit 258 home runs, including his 73 in 2001. I actually started suspecting that Bonds was juicing up as early as 1995, but let's just go with the five-year period when his cap size doubled and he put on about 40 pounds of muscle. Would you give me 15 home runs a year as result of the juice?

That's 75 home runs.

Would it be outrageous to suggest that Clemente could have added 10 to 15 home runs a year for the last five years of his career if he had been willing to go to the needle?

If you consider all the extenuating circumstances, the significance of that huge gap between Clemente's and Bonds' power numbers shrinks almost as much as Barry's testicles.

Beyond all that — I saw them both play.

The real, pre-steroid Barry Bonds did nothing better than Clemente.

He wasn't a better hitter for average and there's plenty of evidence to suggest that, faced with the distances that Clemente faced for 15½ seasons, Bonds wouldn't have had a significant (if any) edge in career home runs.

But, with all due respect, I will say this about Bonds: He is a flaming asshole with, as my friend Bill Hillgrove used to say, flames as long as the Parkway.

CHAPTER 9

SHORT STOP

HOW TO GET A JOB

In the early '80s, I was working for WTAE-TV and we had a kid working for us as a quasi-intern. His father had known somebody who knew me and had asked if his son, who had just graduated from college, could come in to the station to hang around and observe.

I had no problem with it and the kid ended up being a big help.

He wanted to be a TV sportscaster and he had an audition tape that wasn't very good. I worked with him every day and got him to change his delivery and his writing so that he could sound more conversational. That style suited him well and after a few months he was ready to put together a new tape and send it out.

He greatly increased his chances of getting a job by being willing to go anywhere — something that too many young sportscaster wannabes are unwilling to do.

Somehow he heard about an opening for a TV sportscaster in Westlaco, Texas. It was the 167th TV market in the country and about a 3-wood from the Mexican border.

The kid sent his audition tape and a resume and waited for a reply. Before too long, he found out that he was one of three finalists for the job. Of course, he was excited.

One day not long after that he came into the station and said that he didn't get the job and he was pretty bummed.

I asked him the magic question.

"What are you gonna do now?"

"I guess I'll start looking for another opening," he said.

"Nope," I said. "Wrong answer."

The kid tries again — "Call the guy and thank him for considering me?"

My response: "You're half right. Call the guy and ask him who he hired and where he came from. Somebody may have actually left a job somewhere else that's worse than the job in Westlaco."

The kid picks up the phone and makes the call.

The guy on the other end tells him that the guy he hired had been working in Grand Junction, Colorado. The kid makes the call to the news director at the station in Grand Junction and says he's looking for a job.

The news director there says, "Wow. I just lost a guy a couple of hours ago. I need someone right away."

The kid sends his tape and resume and gets his first job in Grand Junction, Colorado, the 180-something TV market in America (for about 12 bucks a week) and he's thrilled.

The kid's name was Alby Oxenreiter, who's now the sports director at WPXI and has been working in the Pittsburgh market for more than 20 years.

In more than 40 years of asking the "magic question" I asked Alby, I have never had anyone answer it correctly.

It seems like such an obvious thing and you would think that everybody in that situation would think to go after the vacancy that was just created by the guy who beat you out for a job.

I once asked the president of a broadcasting school that prided itself in its ability to place its graduates, what he advises his students to do when they apply for a job and get turned down.

He gave me all the usual answers, but not the right one. He was stunned when I told him what I told Alby. He couldn't believe that he hadn't thought of it and he now tells every student to ask that question.

I actually stumbled on to the question when I was trying to get a job in minor league baseball. I was calling every minor league team in the country and asking if they had any openings. If an AAA team had an opening and

I didn't get it, I would assume that the guy who got the job came from an AA or A team and had left an opening behind him.

By the way, I have no idea what happened to the guy who replaced Alby in Grand Junction.

CHAPTER 10

BETTER OR WORSE?

Did I mention that I'm old?

As I write this, I'm about to turn 63 and, even though today's 63 isn't anything like my father's or grandfather's 63, at some point in our lives we reach an age — or at least a point — when we start being accused of always saying that things were better in the good old days when we were young.

I don't know exactly when I reached that point but it was a while ago.

The difference, of course, between being old and being young is that if you're old, you know what it was like in the good ol' days and if you're young, you only think you do.

I was a huge Muhammad Ali fan and my dad used to tell me that Ali would have been a member of Joe Louis' "Bum of the Month" club. I thought that my dad was wrong but I sure couldn't prove it.

He had seen Ali *and* Louis. I had only seen Ali. My only real argument was that my dad was old and thought that everything was better in the good old days.

That may have been true. But I know now that it's also possible that my dad was right.

With that in mind, I thought I'd take a look at what's better and what's worse in our (my?) world right now compared to, say, 35 years ago, when I was in my 20s and couldn't be accused of longing for the good ol' days.

NFL FOOTBALL

BETTER

Come on, let's face it. The players are better. They're bigger, they're stronger and they're faster.

When I was a kid growing up in the '50s and '60s, there were 12 teams. Six in the NFL East. Six in the NFL West. Having 20 more teams is better for everybody. And don't let anybody tell you that because of the addition of 20 teams, the talent is diluted. Our population has increased and more football players are being produced and developed.

The way football is televised is obviously much better. HDTV is one of the greatest inventions of all time and 3D is going to be even more amazing. If more is better, then what we have now is definitely better. In the good ol' days, there was one football game to watch per Sunday. No four o'clock game. No Sunday night, Monday night or Thursday night football.

And the only place I can remember seeing highlights of the Sunday games was on NBC's "Today Show." And they were shown on Tuesday morning because they were on film. The film had to be put on a plane and sent to Philadelphia where it was developed and edited at NFL Films and then sent to New York. So, if you were an NFL fan, you had to spend a day and a half imagining what happened in games after reading about them in the newspaper.

Remember the newspaper?

I'd say the modern NFL fan is better served today by being able to see instant highlights of every game.

Even if they are sometimes voiced over by Linda Cohn.

WORSE

Not everything about the NFL is better than it used to be. Multiple-substitution has turned too many games into chess matches. I don't know about you, but if I want to see a chess match I'll just tune in the Chess Channel and watch a chess match.

I don't remember my dad telling me that one-platoon football was better than the pro football that I grew up with, but I do think it would have been interesting to see Terry Bradshaw stay on the field and play linebacker or strong safety. Imagine Hines Ward as a safety.

I don't think we started hearing about nickel and dime defenses until the early '80s because teams weren't sending out four and five wide receivers on a play.

Why?

Because it would have gotten the quarterback killed. Back then, offensive linemen couldn't use their hands. They had to keep them in at their chests. Running backs and tight ends were needed for pass protection. The rules changes before the 1978 season made it much easier to pass. Maybe too easy. That means a lot more passing and that means a lot more defensive backs and that means a lot more dinking and dunking.

It also means that the offenses have become so complicated that the quarterback has to have a speaker in his helmet to get a play relayed to him from on top of the stadium.

Sorry.

Give me the quarterback popping his head up, surveying the down, the distance and the clock and then popping his head into the huddle and calling a play.

There were no offensive coordinators in the 1960s. That's why you've heard of "Monday morning quarterbacking," but you've never heard of "Monday morning offensive coordinating."

On Monday mornings, fans were at work or school talking about the game that their favorite quarterback had called. His play-calling was every bit as important as his execution.

Now it's all about the offensive coordinators.

That's worse for fans and players.

Offensive coordinators tend to fall in love with their systems and they're constantly trying to force round holes into square pegs. There's no better example of that than what Kevin Gilbride tried to do with Kordell Stewart in 1999.

For a long time, Chuck Noll was his own offensive coordinator and he let Bradshaw call his own game. He didn't hire his first offensive coordinator until he elevated Tom Moore from quarterback coach in 1983.

My favorite example of the overcomplicating of football happened in 1990. The Steelers hired Joe Walton, one of the most respected offensive minds in football, to be their offensive coordinator. There was a lot of excitement in town because people had grown tired of Moore and said that he was boring. (They never accused him of being boring in Indianapolis when he was coordinating Peyton Manning's offense.)

Walton's offense was complicated but we were told that it was going to be much more exciting and a lot more productive. It was *the* topic among the Steelers players for several months leading up to training camp. The players showed us their huge binders with all the plays they had to learn, but they were pumped because they knew it was going to be much better than it was under Moore.

Myron Cope's and Stan Savran's talk shows were abuzz with talk about how much more exciting and high-powered the Steelers offense was going to be.

The players had Walton's offense with them at home to study during the offseason. In training camp, they had the offense drilled into their heads in meeting rooms at St. Vincent College and beaten into them on the field.

The players could be seen walking across campus carrying their huge binders full of all the plays and they gushed about the new offense every time they were asked about it.

Do you know how many touchdowns the Steelers scored in the first four games of the 1990 season?

None.

Zero.

They lost three out of four and had a total of 12 points in the three losses.

I remember saying at the time that after all the excitement and scrutiny that came with Walton's hiring, and after all the binders and all the studying, the Steelers would have scored at least one touchdown if they had let their quarterback, Bubby Brister, go out there and draw plays in the dirt.

Put it this way: They couldn't have scored fewer touchdowns if they had let Mrs. Joe Walton coordinate the offense. (To be fair, the Steelers' offense caught on to Walton's offense enough that Bubby Brister was AFC Offensive Player of the Month for October.)

So, having so much emphasis on the offensive coordinators, in my opinion, has made the game worse, not better. That's not because I'm old. It's because I've seen the game when quarterbacks were calling plays and it was a better game than the one being played today even if today's games are being played by better players. The chess matches notwithstanding, of course.

Then there are the field goals.

I can't tell you how much I've grown to despise the field goal. Kickers are much better today and they have made the game worse. In the good ol' days, kicking a field goal was at least a little bit of an adventure.

Now it's almost as automatic as an intentional walk.

In 2010, the top 20 kickers made 93 percent of their field goal attempts from 20 to 29 yards. They tried 182 and made 164. That means that unless it's late in the fourth quarter and the game is in the balance, if a guy is lining up for a field goal inside 30 yards, it's time to go take a piss.

Same as a commercial break.

In 1958, Paige Cothern of the Los Angeles Rams led the NFL in field goals with 14. He tried 25. That's 56 percent and it was best in the league. Only four other kickers made more field goals than they missed.

In 2010, Sebastian Janikowski of the Oakland Raiders had the most field goals with 33, but he had only an 80 percent conversion rate. Most kickers were at least in the mid-80s with several in the 90s.

The top 10 kickers in the NFL in 2011 made 56 percent of their kicks from *outside the 50*. Exactly the same overall percentage that Cothern had in 1958 and he led the league. When NFL kickers are making field goals at the same rate that NBA free-throw leaders are making their shots, something has to give.

Back in the good ol' days they weren't kicking specialists and they weren't kicking off carpets or field turf and they sure as hell weren't kicking under a dome.

Or in Miami or San Diego.

The NFL is worse now because of the ridiculous success rate of field goal kickers. If your kicker is Paige Cothern and he's barely a 50-50 proposition on a good day, you're a lot more likely to have touchdown on your mind instead of field goal when you get inside the 40.

The modern NFL coach has to start thinking field goal as soon as he crosses the 50-yard line. If he's inside the 30, he has almost a 75 percent chance of getting three points if he doesn't screw it up.

That's why they coach not to screw up.

The NFL decided in 2011 to make up for the boredom of the field goal epidemic by moving kickoffs up to the 35-yard line. They decided kickoffs were too dangerous and wanted to create more touchbacks. So now a boring field goal is more likely to be followed by the most boring play in all of sports, the touchback.

It all translates to less excitement for the fans.

And, despite having better players now, it makes the NFL worse today than it was in the '50s and '60s.

THE STEELERS

BETTER

Unless you *are* an old-timer you think that the Steelers have always been a source of joy and excitement.

Not in the '50s and '60s they weren't. They were the worst team in North American professional sports history until 1972. Since then, they've been one of the best.

I doubt that you hear too many really old-timers talking about the good old days of Steelers football. But I guess those of us who have clear memories of the Steelers of the '70s would have to be pretty old.

As good as the 21st century Steelers have been, I don't know too many of the current Steelers who could have started on those Super Bowl teams.

Troy Polamalu would be one, but he's not a slam-dunk over Donnie Shell.

Is Heath Miller better than Bennie Cunningham? Maybe.

Hines Ward would start in a three wide-receiver set, but he wouldn't put either John Stallworth or Lynn Swann on the bench.

Ben Roethlisberger would not start over Terry Bradshaw and Rashard Mendenhall wouldn't beat out Franco Harris.

The team of the '70s played a different style defense and it's hard to say how they would fit in on the current defense, but styles and schemes aside, there is nobody on the current defense who would have beaten out Jack Lambert, Joe Green, Jack Ham, Mel Blount, Ernie Holmes or Mel Blount.

So is it better or worse to be a Steelers fan in 2011 than it was 35 years ago? I would call it a tie. Both teams went to multiple AFC Championship games and Super Bowls and fans in both eras could go into almost every season thinking the Steelers had a legitimate chance to go to the Super Bowl.

WORSE

The only thing worse about the Steelers is the over-the-top media coverage and the out-of-control, perspective-lacking fans who seem to have become fans of being fans.

In 1972 my buddies and I piled into a car and drove 75 miles west into Ohio (Cambridge, I think) so we could watch the blacked out Steelers on TV against the Kansas City Chiefs. It was when people were just starting to believe that the Steelers, for the first time in 40 years, were one of the best teams in the NFL. The home games weren't on television, so we saw a few of the key games on a motel TV. The motels were full of Steelers fans and when the Steelers would score, you would hear eruptions throughout the building.

On the way home from watching the Steelers beat the Chiefs, my buddy Weezer said, "Enjoy it, boys. It'll never get any better than this."

It didn't.

The Super Bowl seasons were great but, as a fan, it never did get better than that first year when Chuck Noll led the Steelers out of the desert.

We weren't wearing Steelers jerseys that day — just regular human-being clothes. No painted faces on us or any of the other guys in the motel. We were just young football fans who had grown up thinking that the Steelers would never be any good. All of the enthusiasm back then was genuine and spontaneous.

That's not to say that enthusiasm about the Steelers in 2011 isn't genuine. It just seems like the enthusiasm is more about showing your enthusiasm than it is about a real love of football.

MAJOR LEAGUE BASEBALL
BETTER

The players are better. Maybe. Everything else is worse.

WORSE

Where do I begin?

Was Major League Baseball better when I was a kid until I was in my thirties or do I just think it was because I'm an old geezer who thinks everything was better in the old days?

There are four statues at PNC Park right now — Honus Wagner, Roberto Clemente, Willie Stargell and Bill Mazeroski. Thirty or 40 years from now, are my grandkids going to pass by a statue of Andrew McCutchen on their way in to a Pirates game? I watched three of those players play for the Pirates beginning when I was eight years old until I was in my late twenties.

Unless Major League Baseball's economic structure is drastically changed, there isn't a kid alive in Pittsburgh in 2011 who will ever spend more than six or seven years watching a Pirates superstar or future Pirates Hall of Famer.

Baseball Commissioner Bud Selig can sing his parity song all he wants, but if your favorite baseball team doesn't play in a Top 10 TV market, it will take a miracle or near-miracle for it to show up in the World Series.

Thirty-five years ago, the three best franchises in Major League Baseball were in Cincinnati, Pittsburgh and Kansas City. How many of the millions of fans and former fans living in those cities think Major League Baseball is better now than it was then?

The Idiots Who Run Baseball have sentenced baseball to a slow death. It won't happen in my lifetime and may not happen in yours, but it's inevitable. Winning is too dependent on market size and local TV money and, slowly but surely, MLB is losing fans in the medium and small markets.

The trading deadline used to be fun for everybody. Now it's fun for fans in New York, Philadelphia, Boston, Los Angeles and Chicago.

If your team doesn't play in one of 10 or 12 large markets, it's not invited to the free agency party in the offseason. For fans not in those markets, it's like being told to sit at the kids' table for Thanksgiving dinner.

There are a lot more games on TV for fans to watch. In the good ol' days there was one nationally televised game per week — the Saturday "Game of the Week" on NBC. As with the NFL, if more is better, then that's one aspect where Major League Baseball is better. There are games to watch every night and, unlike 35 or 40 years ago, every night you can see highlights of every game.

Of course, some of them are voiced over by Linda Cohn.

They played the first World Series night game in Pittsburgh 40 years ago, in 1971. The overwhelming sentiment was, "It's about time." The NFL had gone primetime on Monday nights the year before and it was time for baseball's most important games to be seen by as many people as possible.

Of course, that first World Series night game started at 7:30. That was the last World Series night game that began before 8. Recently, the games have been starting around 8:40. (Fox planned to start at 8 in 2011). Which means they're over at midnight or later, which means millions of people are choosing sleep over the World Series.

Games used to last two and a half hours, now they're an hour longer. They made up for the stupidity of playing late into the night by scheduling World Series games in November.

The All Star game was must see TV in the '60s and '70s. Now people are asking if the game is more of a pain in the ass than it's worth. That fact that World Series and All Star games were played during the day made them special. The country stopped or at least slowed down a little bit to watch or listen to those games in offices and schools.

Teams from cities like Pittsburgh, Baltimore, Cincinnati and Milwaukee had every bit as much chance to win as teams from the Top 10 markets. The Pirates, Reds, Royals and Orioles dominated the '70s and Milwaukee was one of the best teams in the American League in the early '80s. Was baseball better back then or do I just think it was because I'm old?

THE PIRATES

BETTER

The food at PNC Park is better than the food at Forbes Field.

WORSE

Again, where do I begin? Let's begin with a question. Actually, I'm beginning with two questions but bear with me. Was it better to be a Pirates fan 35 or 40 years ago or do I just think it was because I'm old?

The Pirates finished second in the eight-team National League in 1958. I was nine years old when that season started. From then until I was almost 33 in 1981, I saw the Pirates have five losing seasons and in two of those seasons they were 80-82.

It's been 32 years since the Pirates went to their last World Series. That was half my life ago. In the second half of my life the Pirates have had seven winning seasons.

So, when I say that things were better for Pittsburgh baseball fans in the good ol' days, it's not because I'm old. It's because it's an indisputable fact.

Going back to the 1960s, games were more accessible. You could buy a bleacher seat for a buck — $7.28 in 2010 dollars — and parents allowed their kids to take buses and streetcars to the games at Forbes Field. As opposed to now when they're afraid to let their 10-year-olds go out to the street to get the mail.

My dad worked downtown and would get home from work at about 6:15. On a night when we were going to a game at Forbes Field, he could come home, change clothes, eat dinner and still have plenty of time to drive from the South Hills to Forbes Field in Oakland for an 8:05 game.

That's right. Games started at 8:05 and they were over by 10:30.

Was that better for everybody or am I just old?

Just checking.

So, let's review: Five losing seasons in 23 years or seven winning seasons in 31 years? Which was better? I'll let you decide.

I'm too old.

PITT FOOTBALL

BETTER

I don't know how anyone could say that Pitt football is better now than it was 30 years ago. Is Heinz Field better than Pitt Stadium? It's shinier and it has actual seats as opposed to the benches at Pitt Stadium, so I guess you could say that it is. But it's not on campus and that's still a problem for a lot of people.

WORSE

In the spring of 2011 there was excitement all over Pennsylvania when it was announced that Pitt would be renewing its series with Penn State in 2016. It would only be for two years but it would be the first time the two schools had met since 2000.

What else do you need to know?

As a kid, I don't remember the Pitt-Penn State game being that big of a deal, but by the time I started working in the media, it was as big as it gets.

Beginning in 1976, when Pitt beat Penn State on national TV the day after Thanksgiving, until the mid-'80s, the game was one of the highest-rated games of the year. Locally, it was as big as any Steelers game and it dominated the local media's sports coverage in the week leading up to the game.

In 1981 Pitt went into the game ranked Number One in the country and went up 14-0 before losing 48-14 in what is still the most devastating loss in the history of the program.

The following year both schools went into the game with 9-1 records. Pitt's loss was to Notre Dame and Penn State's was to Alabama. Penn State won and went on to win its first Mythical National Championship.

So, when I say Pitt football was more fun to watch and cover 30 years ago, is that because I'm old or is it because it's an indisputable fact?

COLLEGE FOOTBALL

BETTER

The players are better and there are a lot more games on TV.

WORSE

Pitt played Maine in 2011. What else do you need to know? The BCS and the absurdity of the polls have forced every team to play at least two rent-a-victims a year. Once in a great, great while, a rent-a-victim will pull off an upset. It's so bad that fans and media come to the defense of teams who play rent-a-victims by saying, "You can't play a tough opponent every week." My response has always been, "Why not?"

If all the top teams played 12 real games against real opponents, it wouldn't take a 12-0 season to get into the Mythical National Championship game.

It's one thing for the fans to be suckered into buying tickets to see Pitt play Maine or Penn State play Florida International. It's quite another for the media to accept it and defend it.

There are too many games on TV and it diminishes the value of the games that are on. I kind of liked it in the good ol' days when ABC had to pick one four o'clock game for the second game of the doubleheader.

Every football fan in the country watched Notre Dame-USC or Ohio St.-Michigan. Because they had no choice.

Now, if you don't want to watch Ohio State-Michigan, you can watch Pitt-Maine.

PITT BASKETBALL

BETTER

This one's a no-brainer. Jamie Dixon has turned Pitt's basketball program into one of the best in the country with appearances in the NCAA tournament 11 years in a row and there's no reason to believe that it's going to change.

There has been lots of underachieving in the NCAA tournament, but Pitt basketball has never been better and the Petersen Event Center is one of the best facilities in college basketball. Anybody who tells you Pitt basketball was better in the good ol' days is an old geezer.

WORSE

The Pitt-Duquesne rivalry ain't what it used to be. Those games used to be right up there with the Pitt-Penn State football games for buildup, coverage and excitement. We'll never see that again.

COLLEGE BASKETBALL

BETTER

The players are better.

WORSE

Sixty-four teams in the NCAA tournament are 32 too many. I know I'm in the minority on this one and you can blame it on the fact that I'm old, but since the tournament expanded to 64 teams the 15 and 16 seeds have a combined record of 4-204. Why am I the only person in the country who doesn't find it heartwarming to see Monmouth lose to Duke by 57? Call me crazy, but 4-204 would seem to be an indication that there are teams being invited every year who have no business being there. Or, I guess you could also call me old.

THE PENGUINS

BETTER

Another no-brainer. I don't have to tell you that the Penguins last 25 years have been a thousand times better than their first 20 and the next 10 have the potential to be their best years ever.

WORSE

The Consol Energy Center is a beautiful, new building but I'll take the sight lines and the atmosphere at Civic/Mellon Arena. And I don't think it's because I'm old. You were closer to the action at "The Igloo" and the crowd noise seemed a lot louder.

BOXING

Quick, who's the Heavyweight Champion of the World?

I know it's a Klitchko brother but I would have to Google it to find out which one and get the proper spelling. (I don't care.)

But if I were to say that boxing was much better and more fun to follow 30 to 35 years ago, would that be because I'm old and think everything was better 30 or 35 years ago or would I be right?

When I was 10 I knew that the Heavyweight Champ was Floyd Patterson. I also knew that Sugar Ray Robinson was the welterweight and middleweight champ. In the '70s, the heavyweight division had Muhammad Ali, Joe Frazier, George Foreman, Ken Norton, Ernie Shavers and Ron Lyle, to name a few.

I dare you to name a few 2011 heavyweight contenders.

Forget Ali-Foreman or Ali-Frazier. The Ali-Norton fights were epic. When they fought, it was the top sports story in the country for weeks.

There wasn't a true sports fan in America in 1980 who didn't know that Sugar Ray Leonard was the Welterweight Champion. Everybody knew Roberto Duran when he was Lightweight Champ. When they fought each other for the welterweight title in 1980, it was shown on closed-circuit TV in movie theaters and arenas all over the world. Leonard's fights against Thomas Hearns and Marvin Hagler were right up there with Ali-Frazier.

Boxing still had plenty of problems back then with too many alphabet organizations — WBC, WBA, IBF, etc. — but just about every sports fan knew who was the *real* champion of the various divisions.

I still don't know how Pittsburgh pulled off getting a heavyweight title fight in 1981, but it was a big deal when Larry Holmes fought Renaldo Snipes at the Civic Arena. Don King was in town all week. (He laughed when someone told him that I had said he comes into town a lot to have his hair done at West Penn Power.)

ABC was here with Howard Cosell.

Primetime on Thursday night.

Imagine ABC carrying a boxing match in primetime on a Thursday now.

I can't tell you the last time I watched a boxing match from beginning to end and I couldn't name the titleholder in any of the divisions if my life depended on it.

But don't let anybody tell you that boxing ain't as good as it used to be. If they do, it'll only be because they're old.

And please don't tell me that boxing has been replaced by MMA. I'll buy that when I see MMA on ABC in prime time.

• • •

So, let's review.

Thirty-something years ago, the Pirates were winning their division almost every year. So were the Steelers.

Pitt and Penn State were playing each other every year in one of the highest-rated national telecasts of the season and both regularly came into the game ranked in the top 10.

Pitt and Duquesne were playing each other in basketball — sometimes three times a year — in front of sellout crowds at the Civic Arena.

Boxing was a primetime sport.

Other than that, for the local sports fan everything is better now than it was 30 or 35 years ago.

But what do I know?

I'm old.

CHAPTER 11

SHORT STOP

TATTOOS AND LEISURE SUITS

I have to say I don't get the tattoo thing. It used to be that it was almost only bikers and sailors who had them.

Now they're everywhere.

Tattoos have officially become a fad.

Like shoulder-length hair, bell-bottom jeans and platform shoes in the '60s.

And leisure suits in the '70s.

Remember leisure suits?

Were they ugly enough for you?

It's one thing for a guy to have a heart with his wife's name or a U.S. Marines logo tattooed on his bicep.

And it's even understandable for a woman to have a small tattoo strategically placed somewhere on her body.

But isn't having Brett Keisel's face and famous beard tattooed on your forearm going a little too far?

A guy in Pittsburgh did that recently.

I'm sure his family is proud.

If you're an NFL or NBA player and you don't have a tattoo, you're nobody.

Of course it was the same thing with leisure suits in the '70s.

There was probably a day in the '70s when every athlete in every major pro sport was wearing a leisure suit.

But see, there's a difference. They're not wearing their leisure suits anymore.

Imagine if every guy who made the decision to wear a leisure suit in the '70s made that decision for life.

What if he could never wear anything but leisure suits no matter how much fashions changed?

Picture Joe Greene walking around today in a leisure suit that he couldn't take off.

What's scary is that tattoos are as much of a fad as leisure suits were and 35 years from now, millions of people are going to be doing the equivalent of wearing a leisure suit in 2011.

In 20 years, this country is going to be overrun with buyer's remorse when the 20-somethings with all the tattoos find out that they're wearing the equivalent of a leisure suit.

It's not going to be pretty.

There's a lot of ugliness out there right now.

I wonder, do the tattooed among us really know how ugly most tattoos are? Do the tattooed women know how bad they look and how much worse they're going to look in 20 years?

That initial reaction you get from your tattooed friends when you come back from the tatt parlor isn't the same as the reaction you get when you show them a new pair of shoes.

In 2040, you won't be wearing the same shoes.

If you're a fat woman, take it from a heterosexual man: You're not improving your appearance by putting a huge tattoo on your Ted Kluszewski-like arms. (Ted had the biggest pre-steroid arms in baseball history.)

If you're a woman with fat legs, drawing attention to them by covering your entire calf in tattoos isn't making you more attractive.

And if you're a guy, you really should know that getting a tattoo is no longer a sign of what a rebel you are or how tough you are.

It just shows that you're willing to follow the crowd.

And in 2035 there's a good chance that you're going to be trying to cover them up.

Good luck with that.

May I suggest a leisure suit?

CHAPTER 12

LIFE BY LOTTERY
AND COIN FLIP

I've always been fascinated by free-agent drafts in sports. And I'm not talking about the science of evaluating and drafting football, baseball, basketball and hockey players.

That's interesting, too, but I'm talking about how players' lives are affected forever by what happens on draft day.

Look at Terry Bradshaw.

He will forever be associated with the Pittsburgh Steelers and four Super Bowl wins because he was a no-brainer first overall pick in 1970. Think about how that affected the rest of Bradshaw's life.

But being drafted by the Steelers didn't just affect his life. It changed Melissa Babich's life.

Babich was Miss Teenage America in 1969 and lived in the South Hills of Pittsburgh. If not for their celebrity status, it's unlikely that they would have met, but Bradshaw married Babich in 1972 and they were divorced in 1973.

So the Steelers drafting Bradshaw had a direct and life-long effect on Melissa Babich's family. But Melissa Babich would never have met Bradshaw if a coin that was flipped at the NFL offices in January of 1969 had turned over one more time.

The Steelers and Bears had both finished 1-13 in 1969 and the Steelers won the coin toss to decide who got the first pick.

Forget for a minute about how the history of the Steelers would have changed if that coin had flipped one more time — and it would have been huge. Think about how the Babich family's history would have been changed. Would she have met and married Bobby Douglas, the quarterback who was picked second by the Bears?

And how many people in Chicago, beyond football, were affected by the Steelers winning the coin toss? Douglas, who was one of the best running quarterbacks of all time, wasn't much of a passer and had a mediocre career. If he led the Bears to any Super Bowls, I missed it.

But that coin toss, and the Bears' decision to draft him, put Douglas in the city where Playboy magazine had its headquarters. Douglas married and divorced a Playboy bunny, which, of course, had a lifelong effect on her and her family.

Where would Terry Bradshaw be now if the Bears had won that fateful coin toss? Would he have won any Super Bowls in Chicago? Would he be a network star on a NFL pregame show? Would he have had the opportunity to show his bare ass playing Matthew McConaughey's father in a movie ?

And it's not just the high first-round picks. Think of all of the lives that have been changed by the thousands of decisions made on draft days over the last 50 or 60 years.

On a day in January, 40 years ago, Mike Wagner was sitting somewhere in Illinois wondering if he was going to be drafted.

The Steelers picked him in the 11th round and he ended up playing a major role on the best defense in NFL history and winning four Super Bowl rings. As of this writing, he was still living in Pittsburgh.

What if the Atlanta Falcons, drafting one spot ahead of the Steelers, had picked Wagner instead of Larry Shears, a defensive back from Lincoln College? Think of how different their lives would have turned out. I don't know where Larry Shears is living now, but I know that Mike Wagner wouldn't be living in Pittsburgh.

Dan Schneiss, Bob Pollard, Andy Browder, Albert Davis, Macon Hughes and Vernon Studdard were all picked ahead of Shears and Wagner that day. Where are they now and how did a decision made by some guy sitting in NFL headquarters in New York affect the rest of their lives?

If the Falcons had taken Wagner, would Roger Roitsch be living in Pittsburgh right now? Roitsch was taken by the Broncos right after the

Steelers picked Wagner. He was a defensive tackle from Rice. Would the Steelers have taken him and could he have made the team the way Wagner did and have won four Super Bowl rings?

Mario Lemieux was a no-brainer as the first overall pick in the NHL draft in 1984. What if the Penguins hadn't been smart enough to finish last and be in position to make that pick and the New Jersey Devils had picked first instead of second?

There are four kids named Lemieux who have grown up in Pittsburgh because of what happened on a draft day in 1984. If they all raise their families in Pittsburgh, think of all the human lives, including Lemieux's future grandchildren, who were directly affected by something as otherwise inconsequential as a draft pick.

When the Penguins won their second Stanley Cup in 1992, there were six sheets of hockey ice in the Pittsburgh area. As of this writing there are 36. If Kirk Muller had been the Penguins pick instead of the Devils' pick in 1984, there would still be six sheets of ice in Pittsburgh and four of them would be empty most of the time.

There are very few people on the planet, other than elite athletes, whose lives are directly affected, at 21 years of age, by a decision made by someone they don't know in a room thousands of miles away. And it's about so much more than what they do in football, basketball, baseball or hockey.

A DIFFERENT KIND OF DRAFT

Back in December of 1969, I was hoping I wouldn't be drafted. And it wasn't because I was hoping to sign with the professional team of my choice as a free agent.

I was hoping I wouldn't be drafted into the United States Army and I was part of a lottery that impacted more than 850,000 young men a lot more than any pro sports league's draft ever did.

It was the lottery-by-birthday drawing to determine the order for draft-eligible young men for 1970.

Talk about impacting a kid's life.

This would be a life-and-death lottery for lots of guys. Literally. Get a low number, get drafted and maybe be killed in Viet Nam.

Get a high number and never have to worry about being forced to serve in the military again.

If you were born between 1944 and 1950, your immediate and long-term future was going to be determined by the order in which 366 wooden capsules were pulled out of a drum by a bureaucrat in Washington.

Imagine almost a million guys between the ages of 18 and 25 looking forward to watching their lives change on national TV.

I know the bars in the Oakland section of Pittsburgh were filled with guys watching the drawing on TV. I wasn't there, but my two friends, Goose and Tom were. I missed the "show" because I had to work that night at Giant Eagle while the rest of my life was being determined on national TV.

Goose, Tom and I had a plan.

If we all got high numbers and no longer had to worry about the deferment for staying in school, we were going to head for California. Keep in mind that all guys between the ages of 19 and 25 had been dealing with worrying about the military draft for a long time. Especially the older guys.

There were student deferments and deferments for being married with a kid. There were also deferments for teachers. I know a lot of guys who took up teaching because they knew it would keep them from getting drafted and sent to Vietnam. I also know a lot of guys who did whatever it took to stay in college for no other reason than to get the college deferment.

But after the lottery, life was going to very simple. Under 195, you got drafted; over 195 and you were home free.

I hurried home after work because I knew Goose and Tom were going to be calling me from the bar with the results.

The phone rang.

I took a breath and picked it up.

And heard two drunken idiots singing "California here we come..."

Tom got 347.

Goose got 254.

I got 244.

It wasn't even close. Unless World War III broke out, we were never going to have to worry about getting drafted again. If we had drawn 144, 147 and 154, our three lives would have been drastically changed and the quality of the United States Army would have been drastically reduced.

The unlucky guys who got low numbers started scrambling. They tried to pull strings to get into the National Guard or the reserves. A lot of guys, to avoid being drafted into the army, enlisted in the Navy or the Air Force. Many of them ended up in Vietnam anyway.

There's no way of knowing how many ways American history would have been changed if those capsules had been drawn out of that drum in a different order, but there was a guy across the pond in Britain at the University of Oxford who may not have seen his number drawn on TV but must have thrown a party when he got the news.

Bill Clinton drew a 311.

He had avoided the military draft a year earlier by promising the head of the ROTC at the University of Arkansas that if he were allowed to take advantage of his Rhodes Scholarship and go to Oxford, he would go to grad school and sign up for ROTC.

After Clinton got the 311, he no longer had to worry about getting drafted, so he blew off the ROTC. That move became a major campaign issue in 1992.

If Clinton gets a 111 instead of a 311, he would have been faced with a decision to stay in the UK and dodge the draft or come home and serve. But because of how the capsules were drawn on December 1, 1969, Bill Clinton was on his way to the presidency of the United States.

Tom, Goose and I were on our way to Miami.

I don't know what happened to our California plan, but Miami beat the hell out of Da Nang.

CHAPTER 13

SHORT STOP

LITTLE MILES

In May of 2006, I was assigned by KDKA-TV to pay a visit to the home of the Steelers' new Number One draft pick, Santonio Holmes. That meant a trip to Belle Glade, Florida.

Before I left, sports producer Mike Vukovcan gave me a list of names and numbers of people I would be interviewing, including Holmes' mother, high school football and track coaches and other people who had known him as a kid.

I also had a number for Holmes' stepfather "Little Miles."

We flew into West Palm Beach and made the drive west to Belle Glade, a small town in the middle of sugarcane country that has been affectionately referred to as Muck City.

Why was it known as Muck City?

Because there's a lot of muck around. That's where sugarcane is grown — in the muck. Most of the people who lived in town were poor and black.

Holmes' mother, Patricia Brown, lived in an old, ramshackle house that's probably no bigger than your living room, dining room and kitchen and that's if you live in a normal-sized house.

We had to wait until early afternoon to pay her a visit because she worked in the cornfields from about 4 a.m. to noon every day.

I don't remember what she did there but I know it didn't involve air conditioning. This was one hard working, impressive woman. I'd say she was in her late 30s to early 40s. She appeared to have about half of her teeth.

As I was talking to her about Santonio, a man came through the front door and introduced himself, "Hi. I'm Little Miles."

Eventually, I got around to asking him about what Santonio was like as a kid and all the other routine questions. I also learned that he was really worried about going to his stepson's NFL games because he had never flown before. And, like Patricia, he asked a lot about the cold weather and wondered how anybody could stand it.

Miles seemed like a nice guy with a quick smile that showed a lot of missing teeth. After things loosened up, I said, "So, where's Big Miles?" He said, "There is no Big Miles, just me, Little Miles," and I told him that I just assumed that if he was Little Miles there must have been a Big Miles.

Then I asked him what his real name was. He said, "Little Miles." I said, "No, I meant your real name."

"Little Miles."

I tried again. "No, seriously, what's your first name?"

He said, "Little."

Then he laughed and took out his Florida driver's license. Right there next to his picture was his name: Little Miles.

This guy had gone through life with "Little" as a first name.

I never thought to ask him what his middle name was and, thinking back on it, I'm guessing that he either didn't have one or it made less sense than Little. Otherwise, if someone had stuck you with Little as a first name, wouldn't you eventually opt for the middle name to avoid the confusion?

I enjoyed meeting the people who raised Santonio Holmes and after interviewing his former coaches and mentors, I came back to Pittsburgh with a pretty good story.

I saw Holmes shortly after that at Steelers mini-camp, introduced myself and told him about meeting his mother and his stepfather.

He half-looked at me, grunted something and walked away.

His mother and Little would have been disappointed.

I got a first impression that still sticks with me today.

Punk.

CHAPTER 14

DELIVERING THE SPORTS

I started delivering sports news in 1959 when I was 11 years old. That's when I became a Pittsburgh Press paperboy. Maybe that's where my journalism seed was planted. I don't remember thinking about it at the time, but maybe, somewhere in my subconscious, I developed an affection and an appreciation for being one of the first to know.

In the days before the Internet and the four and five o'clock TV news, there were many times when I would be in charge of breaking big news on the doorsteps of my 52 customers on Blue Jay and Cardinal drives.

There are no paperboys now, of course.

If you have kids or grandkids, it's probably hard for you to imagine an 11-year-old being given the responsibility of delivering newspapers. For a long time now, our newspapers have been delivered by adults in cars.

Apparently, kids either became too lazy or parents became over-protective and a great American tradition gradually faded away.

I knew the tradition and the future of American men were in trouble in 1983 when, on a perfectly sunny summer day, I looked out the window and saw our paperboy being driven on his route by his mommy. Not only did she have the papers sitting on the open tailgate of the family station wagon, she was actually stopping the car and taking the papers to the door.

At first, I hoped, for the sake of my country and my gender, that this was a one-time thing — maybe the kid was in a hurry to go somewhere or had some kind of minor injury. But it wasn't.

It was a daily occurrence.

This perfectly healthy 11- or 12-year-old boy was somehow incapable of delivering his papers on foot and had to be driven by his mother. See, this kind of defeated the purpose of being a paperboy. The idea was, or at least, was supposed to be, that the kid was given the responsibility and he learned the meaning and value of being on time and being dependable.

This kid didn't have a paper route, his mother did.

If you take a trip around Birdland — the neighborhood where I grew up in Scott Township — you'll notice that at least 90 percent of the homes have only one garage. That's because 90 percent of the families owned one car and mom wasn't the one who got to drive it during the day.

So, even if mothers had been inclined to drive their paperboy sons around, they didn't have the wheels. That also meant that moms weren't available to drive their kids to karate instructions, swimming pools, arts-and-crafts classes and whatever else modern mothers are driving them to nowadays.

That's why we had so many kids available for our after-school pickup games. If you were a Press paperboy, you worked in the afternoon and that meant figuring out a way to get your pickup baseball, football and basketball games in without being late with the paper.

I actually had to wear a watch.

Do you know any 11-year-olds who wear a watch?

I was late with the paper a lot. But I also learned the value of moving quickly and I became really good at folding and throwing a newspaper. (Folding a newspaper for throwing is another lost art, by the way. I'll bet you can't find someone under the age of 40 who can do it.)

Something else I learned the value of because I was a paperboy — money. There were only a few paper routes available and the kids who had them quickly became recognized as being "rich."

From the time I was in sixth grade, I've had an appreciation for the good feeling of having my own money jingling in my pocket. The Press paid me 1½ cents per daily paper and 2½ cents for each Sunday paper. Fifty-two customers meant $5.98 a week, plus tips. A dime was a big tip.

My salary came out to about a buck a day. That's right. I had to work seven days a week. Parents who tried to get away with making their 11-year-old work seven days a week now would be charged with child abuse. (Seven dollars in 1958 would be equal to $52 in 2011 dollars.)

Then there was collecting.

All paperboys hated collecting. That's when you would take your collecting cards with the little tear-away tickets on them, knock on the customer's front door and, when it opened, say, "Collecting." I actually remember saying that every time the door opened and neither I nor the customer thought it was strange.

When I started delivering the Press in 1958, it was 62 cents a week, seven cents daily and 20 cents on Sunday. A couple of years later it went up to 67 cents a week. My route was only one street away and it was like having my own ATM machine. If someone wanted to go to the Pirates game, I would look through my collecting cards, find someone who owed me for three weeks and knock on their door.

"Collecting."

They would pay me my $2.01 and that would be all I would need for a $1 bleacher seat, a popcorn and a coke.

For some reason, I didn't feel abused when my friends would just hold out their hand and have their old man put two dollar bills in it — without having to say "Collecting." I think I liked demanding it better than having to ask for it.

When I would be greeted by a customer who wanted to know why the paper was late, I'd use it as a good lesson in customer relations. I'd lie and say that the truck was late.

Of course, there was one kid who ruined it for everybody else.

Lou Duke, the son of a military man and a future Pennsylvania State cop, was never late when he delivered his papers. He'd be waiting for the Press truck at the drop-off spot and would practically catch the bundle of papers before they hit the ground.

He was a popular, nice kid doing the right thing and keeping his commanding officer at home happy, but the other paperboys in the neighborhood made fun of his earnestness a lot. He also annoyed us because his work ethic made it harder for us to lie about the truck being late. We never knew if our customers might have seen him delivering his papers an hour before we showed up with theirs. Lou Duke would actually get upset when the papers really were late.

Of all the headlines that I saw when I opened up my bundle of freshly printed Pittsburgh Presses, I can only remember two. One was the announcement that the Surgeon General of the United States had determined that cigarette smoking caused lung cancer. That was a bombshell for a lot of reasons, not the least of which was that I had started smoking about six months earlier.

It seemed like everybody smoked in those days, including both of my parents and my parish priest, and I thought we were all doomed. The only other story I remember jumping out at me was one that I was expecting. It was November 22, 1963. I was anxious to see the headline about the assassination of President Kennedy.

Earlier that day, around two o'clock, I was sitting in Spanish class at South Hills Catholic High School when we heard the principal, Brother Alfred, on the P.A. system: "Attention students. I have some very bad news to report. Our president has been shot."

Talk to anyone who was in school that day and he'll tell you (it was an all-boys school) that he thought Ferb Gannon had been shot. Ferb was our student body president and was known to be a little bit of a wild man. Not only that, Ferb, who had been elected vice president at the end of the previous school year, had been awarded the position when the kid who was elected president was arrested over the summer.

After Brother Alfred made it clear that it was President Kennedy who had been shot, he dismissed us all. Of course, everybody was stunned and trying to make sense of it as we headed for the front of the room. Lou Duke happened to be in that class with me and I'll never forget what he said as we met near the door. I could see that he was especially upset and when we made eye contact he said, "Boy are papers going to be late today."

Talk about dedication.

CHAPTER 15

QUOTES FROM THE UNFAMOUS

O ur next-door neighbors growing up in Scott Township were a nice childless couple named Jen and Emil. (No last name needed.)

Emil was a retired carpenter and Jen worked in a meatpacking plant. Jen was sort of like an aunt to us and it was understood that, if we got out of line, she was *expected* to correct us.

It wasn't unusual back then for adults to correct each other's kids. I'm pretty sure that has changed.

Anyway, Emil and Jen were Pittsburghers through and through. Emil was always chomping on a cigar and Jen was rarely without a cigarette. They were good, hard-working, blue-collar Americans.

Quite a buzz was created in the neighborhood when word got out that Jen and Emil were going to take a trip to California. Remember, this was the late 1950s and going to California was still a big deal.

They were gone for a couple of weeks and when they returned, everybody was eager to hear about their trip. That's when Jen, in her deep, smoky voice and thick Pittsburgh accent said this to my mother:

"Kay, I'm tellin' ya. California is a wild, wild, wild *taahn.*"

CHAPTER 16

"FORT NEVER LOSE"

I became a hockey convert in 1982.

Prior to that, I was strictly a baseball and football guy who covered basketball when I had to and enjoyed seeing games in person but would have been OK if basketball ceased to exist. I didn't dislike hockey, but I had a hard time appreciating it on the same level as football and baseball — probably because I had never played it.

I stopped playing organized football and baseball when I was 13, but I was a pretty good playground player in both sports and could more than hold my own against my friends who played high school and college football.

I had been on skates once in my life.

Everything changed when my son Brett started playing hockey. He actually started with learn-to-play hockey clinics in 1980 when he was about 8½.

In 1982 he was ready to play on a team and that's when I realized what I had missed when I was a kid. I would leave every one of his practices shaking my head and asking myself why I never played the game.

The answer was pretty simple, actually. There weren't any ice rinks around when I was a kid and the Penguins didn't show up until a year after I graduated from high school.

Notice I said *practices*. I couldn't believe how much fun the hockey practices were and I noticed that it didn't matter to the kids that they were taking place at five in the morning.

The games, of course, were even better. They were usually played much later in the day. Usually around 7:30 a.m. In places like Greensburg and Beaver County, a long way from our home in Mt. Lebanon.

I noticed right away that Brett never complained about having to get up at 4:15 in the morning and I knew that, if I had been trying to get him up in the middle of the night to go to baseball, basketball or football practice, I would have had a fight on my hands at least half the time.

A couple of years later, when he was able to get up and dress himself, I told him to wake me when he was ready. I was doing the 11 p.m. sports in those days and wasn't getting home until after midnight. I can't tell you how many times I went to bed hoping against hope that he would forget to set or just turn off his alarm and blow off practice.

It never happened. Not once. And there was no way he was going to blow off a game.

I get the exact same feeling about missing out on hockey now when I see how much fun my four grandsons have when they're playing. I never see a practice or a game when I don't envy them and wish I had been exposed to the sport when I was their age.

Meanwhile, when I go to their youth baseball games, I feel sorry for them because they look so bored most of the time.

Go to a hockey game played by 9- and 10-year-old kids and you'll see a hockey game. There will be passes made, shots on goal and good saves. There also will be a lot of falling down, but you will actually see something that resembles hockey. Go to a baseball game being played by the same kids and you'll see a lot of kids standing around.

There will be one or two kids on each baseball team who can actually play. But most of them can't catch, throw or hit and have no business being on a baseball field and especially no business wearing a baseball uniform.

I have a feeling that youth baseball has been turned upside down. It used to be that you didn't try out for a baseball team until you could, you know, *play baseball.* Maybe the fact that we put the kiddies in their uniforms before they learn how to play is another example of the feminization of America.

The difference between youth hockey and youth baseball is that young hockey players spend much more time practicing and going to clinics than they spend pretending to play.

And that's what most 9-year-old baseball players are doing. They're pretending to play baseball.

There's no hockey equivalent of a walk or hiding in right field. Eventually the puck is going to come to you and you're going to have to do something with it. And when a 9-year-old hockey player comes off the ice after a game, he's soaked in sweat. A 9-year-old baseball player comes off the field relieved that the game's over and he's free to go have some fun.

My grandsons (left to right) Wyatt (8), Jake (8), Luke (10) and Gunnar (10), will get up at 6 a.m. to play hockey. I doubt that any of them would care if baseball disappeared at 6 a.m. tomorrow.

I base that opinion on having watched my grandsons play a hockey game in the morning and a baseball game in the afternoon. I don't know how it would be possible for a parent who never played hockey and was never a fan of the sport, *not* to be converted by having a son on the ice.

WELCOME TO "FORT NEVER LOSE"

As impressed as I was by my exposure to youth hockey, I was still mostly a football-baseball guy when it came to college and pro games that I watched or covered in my job as a sports anchor/reporter at WTAE.

That all changed on Long Island in April of 1982.

I was there in the Nassau County Coliseum for the Penguins 4-3 overtime loss to the Islanders in Game 5 of a five-game playoff series that began with the Penguins losing the first two games on the road by a combined score of 15-3.

After those first two losses, the Penguins' owner Ed DeBartolo released this statement:

"No one is more upset and disappointed with the play of the Pittsburgh Penguins than me. I am not attending Saturday night's playoff game and I empathize with you fans who have decided not to come to the Civic Arena tomorrow night. Should fans who have purchased tickets feel a refund is warranted, the Pittsburgh Penguins will comply with that wish."

Roll that around in your brain for a while and try to picture it happening in 2011. This is, as far as I know, still the only time in American history that an owner of a major sports franchise has offered fans a refund because of his team's poor play.

Fewer than 200 fans took DeBartolo up on the offer and more than 14,000 showed up for Game 3 at Civic Arena.

I was there.

The fans were standing and chanting "Let's Go Pens" for several minutes before the Penguins came on the ice and they gave the team a long standing ovation after the National Anthem. It was one of the most electrifying moments I've ever experienced in an arena.

As most good Penguins fans know, the Penguins won Games 3 and 4. Keep in mind that they did this against the New York Islanders, who had won the two previous Stanley Cups and would eventually win two more.

And if there weren't enough ingredients to make that third game memorable, it took a goal by Rick Kehoe four minutes into overtime to win it. The crowd almost blew the roof off the Arena when it went in.

Nobody had given the Penguins a chance when the series started and not even their owner gave them a chance after the first two games. But now they were tied 2-2 and headed for Game 5 on Long Island.

Even though the Penguins hadn't been a high priority when it came to which teams to cover, everybody in the local media had known for a long time that hockey players were the most media-friendly of all the major sports. That's what makes covering a good hockey playoff series so enjoyable. The players are much more accessible and they have a much better understanding of the media's job than other athletes.

Imagine this:

It's 1979 and the Steelers are getting ready to play the Houston Oilers in the AFC Championship game. It's about an hour before game time and Chuck Noll pops out of the Steelers locker room, walks up to a reporter, shakes his hand and says, "Wait 'till you see what he have in store for (Dan) Pastorini today."

I can guarantee you that scenario never happened.

On April 13, 1982, I had just done my 6 o'clock live shot for WTAE and I was standing outside the Penguins locker room in the Nassau County Coliseum, when Penguins head coach Eddie Johnston popped his head out the door, spotted me and came over and shook my hand.

"Wait 'till you see what we're gonna do with (Bryan) Trottier tonight," Johnston said. Then he went on for another minute or two explaining what the plan was for Game 5 and I just nodded. I had no idea what he was talking about, but that didn't matter. I was stunned that he would want to share that information with a microphone puke like me a half an hour before the biggest game of his coaching career.

It also was a major event in my hockey conversion.

Here's what E.J. was up against: The Islanders had won 54 and lost only 16 in the regular season and they were 23-2 in their last 25 games at Nassau County Coliseum, which had become known around New York as "Fort Never Lose." The last time he had been in the building his team had lost two games and been outscored 15-3. Now he was trying to beat the Islanders for the third time in a row.

I had never experienced an atmosphere at a hockey game that came close to what I saw on Long Island that night. It was a new building filled with over 15,000 people, all of whom felt that there was no way their team could lose.

At the Civic Arena I was used to Vince Lascheid's organ getting the crowd fired up with his *bomp... bomp... bomp... bomp* and the "Let's Go Pens" cheer. At "Fort Never Lose" they actually played loud music. It was the first time I had ever heard "We Will Rock You" at a sporting event. It had to be unbelievably intimidating to the Penguins. I had also never seen an arena go from as loud to as quiet, which it did when the Penguins scored to take a 3-1 lead.

The Islanders cut the lead to 3-2 on a power play goal set up by a Bryan Trottier dive. But the Penguins were still holding on thanks to spectacular goal tending from Michel Dion, who had been standing on his head since Game 3, and whatever it was Eddie Johnston was doing to contain Trottier.

But with just under 2:30 to go, Penguins defenseman Randy Carlyle, with no one within 15 feet of him, went to retrieve a puck bouncing off the rear boards. It took a "Penguins Curse" bounce and somehow went over his stick and on to Islander forward John Tonelli's stick and he snapped it past Dion to send the game into overtime.

That goal created the loudest roar I had ever heard at a sports event in my life and the fans were singing, "We Will, We Will ROCK You."

Mike Bullard had a chance to win the game for the Penguins in overtime but he shot the puck over the net on a breakaway. At 6:19 Tonelli scored again to end it.

The place went nuts, of course, and it was the first time I had ever heard Queen's "We Are the Champions" in a sports arena.

While the Islanders were celebrating at one at end of the ice, Michel Dion was lying face down with his head inside the goal line. He lay there for several minutes before joining the handshake line. The Islanders fans gave the Penguins a standing ovation when they went off the ice.

It was, without a doubt, one of the greatest performances ever by a Pittsburgh team. It has gotten lost in all the great performances by teams that ended up with championships. If the Penguins had been able to hold on to their lead for 2 minutes and 21 seconds more, it would have been one of the greatest comebacks and biggest upsets in sports history.

I think it's pretty safe to say that no other team will ever get a chance to try to come back from two games to none after its owner offers its fans a refund.

As the Penguins were leaving the ice, I was hustling to get to their locker room. (I'm pretty sure that I was the only Pittsburgh TV guy there.) I went from ear-piercing singing and screaming to dead silence.

I told the cameraman to start rolling before we went in the locker room because I had a feeling we were going to see something dramatic.

Nobody was moving and nobody was making a sound. Players were still in their uniforms, sitting in front of their stalls and staring at the floor. Michel Dion was lying motionless on his back with his feet propped up on his locker stool.

The reaction that I received in that locker room was also a big part of my conversion. Every player that I approached was willing to talk. They couldn't have been more professional.

Michel Dion, with his French accent, said, "I've been in emotional periods like that before. I've had a few like that in my life. Some of them have turned out against myself. No way to describe what it does to your heart. It's like it's shattering in a thousand pieces.

There's tremendous joy knowing that you played so strong and so hard … just about gave the best team in the world the roughest and toughest series that they've been involved in in the last five years. Knowing that, deep down in their heart on the other side, they know that it could have been ours just as well."

When I left that building that night I was a lifelong hockey fan. I started trying to imagine what it would be like to see and hear in Civic Arena what I had seen and heard in the Nassau County Coliseum.

I would have to wait until 1991 to find out.

On my first day back to work after the game, I ran into Myron Cope in the newsroom and he asked me how my trip was. I told him that the game was one of the greatest sporting events I had ever seen.

Myron looked at me as though I was nuts.

He couldn't imagine feeling that way about any game that didn't involve the Steelers.

I don't think he ever converted.

CHAPTER 17

QUOTES FROM THE UNFAMOUS

I love Canadians.

I know it's ridiculous to make this kind of a generalization, but they're friendlier than Americans. They're not tougher, but, because of their location on the planet, they may be a little hardier.

It was an unusually cold day in late October and I was walking on the sidewalk in Port Colborne, Ontario.

A guy with his hat down over his ears and his collar up looks me — a total stranger — in the eye, smiles and says:

"Brrrr, eh?"

Those two words sum up the essence of an entire country. They should be printed on the back of all Canadian currency, kind of like our "In God We Trust."

CHAPTER 18

FIXES

N obody asked me, but I'm here with solutions for what ails sports in 2011.

NFL
TOO MANY FIELD GOALS

Let's face it, there are way too many field goals because field goals have become too easy to make. There was a period in my lifetime when a guy could lead the NFL in field goals with a 56 percent success rate.

In 2011, NFL field goal kickers make their kicks at an 82 percent rate. Several were over 90 percent in 2010. If you take field goals out of the equation, NFL games in the '40s and '50s were more high-scoring than they are now. Because field goals are so easy to make, NFL coaches find their sphincter muscles puckering up when they get inside their opponents' 30-yard line. They know they have close to a 90 percent chance of getting three points if they don't turn it over.

When they're inside the 15, their chance of getting three is 97 percent. Come on.

Fans deserve better than that, don't they?

Soccer-style kickers and perfect kicking conditions have changed the field goal from a 50-50 proposition to almost a slam-dunk. All you need to know is that the only kicker in the Pro Football Hall of Fame is

Jan Stenerud, who spent most of his 20-year career with the Kansas City Chiefs. Going into the 2011 season, Stenerud, who retired in 1985, was ranked the 104th most accurate kicker in NFL history at 68 percent.

Modern day kickers have passed the NFL by.

The solution is simple. Get rid of the goal posts.

OK. I can see where some people might consider that a slightly radical solution. So how about narrowing the goal posts? The uprights are 18-feet 6-inches apart right now. How about squeezing them into 12-feet 6-inches?

Would you give me 15 feet?

Maybe coaches sitting on their opponent's 15-yard line and looking at a fourth and two would begin to think that going for the first down was a safer proposition. What would you rather see, two teams digging in at the 15 on a fourth and two or a 185-pound soccer player kicking a glorified extra point?

GUTLESS PUNTING

Another fairly new problem is NFL coaches punting from inside their opponent's 40-yard line. I've seen NFL coaches punt from inside the 35. How gutless is that? And is it boring enough for you?

If I owned an NFL team, on the day that I hired my head coach, I would tell him that if I ever saw him punt from inside the 40, he would be fired. That may be a little radical for some and might not catch on with the other owners, so how about this?

If you make the gutless, stupid decision to punt from inside your opponent's 40-yard line and the ball goes into the end zone, your opponent starts at his own 40 and not the 20.

THE CFL WAY

The NFL could learn a few things from the Canadian Football League. For starters, it could adapt the 20-second play clock. Why do quarterbacks who have speakers in their helmets (another thing that needs to go) need all that time to get a play off?

The CFL has a three-minute warning at the end of each half instead of a two-minute warning. And the clock stops after every play and doesn't start again until the ball is placed by the official.

That means a lot more late comebacks and it means a lot less genuflecting. Why should fans have to sit and watch a quarterback go down on one knee three times in a row? Would you rather see that or a quarterback being forced to get first downs if he wants to keep the ball away from his opponent?

A FUMBLE IS A FUMBLE

The NFL should go back to making a fumble a fumble. If you hit the ground and the ball comes out, you fumbled. Call me crazy, but I consider a fumble more exciting than a referee looking at replays to determine if a runner's knee made contact with the top of a blade of grass 1/32nd of a second before he lost the ball.

The play shouldn't be over until the ball carrier hits the ground and shows that he still has possession of the ball.

NO TOUCHBACKS

The NFL is doing everything possible to prevent kickoff returns. The CFL makes it impossible for a touchback to happen. There's no such thing up north. The NFL is doing it to reduce the possibility of injury. Eliminating tackling would do that, too.

Fans would be better served if the NFL did a better job of drug testing. That would cause players to shrink and that would do more for safety than eliminating the kickoff. Another way to increase safety would be to limit the size of players' facemasks. Go back to the one-bar mask and watch how many of the "tough" guys who make a living by launching into ball carriers with their helmets disappear.

TOO MANY COMMERCIALS

Have advertisers become more stupid over the years? Do the people running the major TV networks know that we have remote-control channel changers?

If so, why do they present their commercials the same way they did in 1972?

Let's say you're watching the Steelers and the Ravens on CBS. It's the first quarter and the Steelers' first drive has stalled. They punt. Don't you and every other person watching the game know that there is a commercial coming?

Do you know anybody who *doesn't* either immediately change the channel to watch the game on Fox or hit the mute button? OK, so some people may go to the bathroom or the kitchen, but nobody's watching 2½ minutes of commercials.

What if you were, say, Miller Beer, and you had paid $100,000 for a 30-second ad and you saw that your ad fell in the middle of that 2½-minute cluster that nobody saw? Would you think you were getting your money's worth?

In 1972, nobody had a remote and nobody got up out of their chair to walk across the room and change the channel when the commercials started. If you were an advertiser, you could be pretty confident that your ad was reaching its intended audience.

The NFL could shorten the length of its games and the advertisers could get a bigger bang for their buck by showing fewer commercials. Instead of running the ads in the same spot every time, when every NFL fan armed with a remote knows they're coming, sneak up on the viewers by dropping 20-second commercials in during the game. After a long pass, roll the commercial.

There is already someone on the sideline whose job is to tell the referee when it is OK to resume play. That person could hold up the game for an extra five seconds if the 20-second commercial is still running as the teams are getting ready to break the huddle.

The networks could actually charge as much for the 20-second commercial as they do for a 60-second commercial because they could assure the advertisers that more people would see it.

It wouldn't be hard for ad agencies to come up with creative, entertaining, 20-second commercials and fans would be spared those touchdown-2½ minutes of commercials-kickoff-2½ minutes of commercials sandwiches that act as a messages to change the channel.

Games would be shorter, advertisers would get more eyeballs and the networks would hold their audiences.

MAJOR LEAGUE BASEBALL

SALARY CAP

The salary cap's not going to happen any time soon because the Idiots

Who Run Baseball came up with a revenue sharing plan that allows the markets outside the Top 10 to make money while still leaving the mega-market teams with enough local TV money to make it impossible for the smaller market teams to compete for available players.

Several years ago, I was told by former Pirates owner Kevin McClatchy that teams like the Pirates had the power to refuse to allow visiting teams to televise their games. He said prior to the last Collective Bargaining Agreement that the small markets were going to use that power and demand that the mega-market teams split their TV money with them 50-50 when they play at PNC Park. McClatchy and the other owners caved when the mega-market guys promised them enough revenue sharing to make a profit.

So, for Pittsburgh, barring a miracle, there is no real hope that the Pirates could become a long-term contender.

SELL THEIR SHIRTS

I do have one suggestion to help close the revenue gap between the haves and have-nots. Allow the have-nots to advertise on their uniforms. I know that would cause baseball purists to have nervous breakdowns, but the competitive purity of baseball disappeared a long time ago. The teams in the mega-markets would have to agree not to advertise on their uniforms as a way of giving the have-nots a chance to make up for the difference in revenue from local TV. Major advertisers could buy ads on jerseys or hats. Those ads would be seen by millions of people over the course of a season and they would be most beneficial to advertisers when the have-nots were playing in one of the haves' ball parks.

NO MORE DH

Major League Baseball also needs to get rid of the DH. It's a stupid rule that allows fat, out-of-shape guys to claim to be baseball players when they are really only baseball *hitters*.

Finding a place in the field for an all-hit, no-field player should be part of the game. And a fat guy in right field can provide almost the same potential for offense as a designated hitter.

NBA

I DON'T CARE

I don't care.

NHL

START SOONER, END SOONER

Try suggesting to someone associated with the NHL that the season should start in September and end by May 1 and you will see some serious eye-rolling, maybe hear some loud gagging.

The answer you will get is that September is too early for hockey and they can't imagine competing with football in September.

This is a league that is obviously OK with playing its most important and compelling games in mid-June.

Sometimes in Florida or California.

If a Canadian hockey fan had gone into a coma in the '50s and awakened in the early 21st century and you told him that the Stanley Cup Finals were being played the second week of June, he would think you were crazy.

He might ask to go back into a coma because he wouldn't want to live in a world that had gone that mad.

The NHL regular season usually covers 27 weeks. If they were to start on, say, September 12, and play their 82-game schedule over 27 weeks, they could start the first playoff games on March 15.

It would still be winter.

There would be snow on the ground in many places.

It would seem like it made sense to be playing hockey.

The Stanley Cup Finals would be over by May 15 — sooner if they would get back to playing games every other night.

The best games of the season would be played in March and April — months when most of the real hockey fans are still spending most of their time inside, especially at night.

As opposed to playing most of the best games of the season in May and June when hockey fans, most of whom live where it's, you know, cold, are anxious to get out of the house and not sit in front of their TVs.

Imagine if the NFL played the Super Bowl on June 15. Do you think it would get anything close to the ratings it gets in February when 80 percent of North America is housebound?

Forget worrying about competing with the NFL and college football in September. You're competing with them in October, too. By the middle of September, people in the Northeast are thinking about cold weather sports, not water skiing.

And forget about competing with the NCAA basketball tournament. Hockey fans watch hockey and basketball fans watch basketball. Believe it or not, the NCAA basketball tournament doesn't get huge ratings.

To me, it's a no-brainer. Do you want to play your most important and compelling games when it feels like you should be watching hockey or do you want to play them when it feels like you should be at the beach?

GET AWAY FROM THE BEACH
GET AWAY FROM THE DESERT

It was a nice try by Gary Bettman. Shortly after he became NHL Commissioner, he made it his mission to put the NHL in places where water never freezes.

A team that was in Winnipeg, Manitoba, moved to Phoenix.

Minnesota's team moved to Dallas.

Hartford's team moved to Raleigh.

Quebec's team moved to Denver.

Denver is the only one that made sense.

The Stars won a Cup in Dallas and they draw pretty well, so you might be able to make a case for keeping a team there.

Same is true of Raleigh.

But being the radical that I am, I want the entire South and Southwest vacated. Hockey in Miami? Hockey in Tampa?

Come on.

Those franchises have had their moments, but you can't just go by sold-out buildings in long playoff runs. Look at the TV ratings. They're embarrassing in Miami, Tampa, Phoenix, Nashville, San Jose and Los Angeles.

Move them north and move them to Europe. Milwaukee should have a team, so should Quebec City. Form a European Division with teams in Stockholm, Helsinki, Moscow and Prague. It would give the league a more exotic flavor and make for some really interesting telecasts.

Scheduling could be worked out so that North American teams only travel there once or twice a season. Night games over there would be day games here. It could be done and whatever the logistical problems were, it would make more sense than hockey in Phoenix or Miami.

UNLIMITED POWERPLAY GOALS

Why allow a team that is playing with the man advantage to score only one goal? Fans like power plays. Make the penalized team kill the entire two minutes. It would greatly increase scoring and it would keep teams in the game longer.

FORGET THE POINTS

The NHL had to be dragged kicking and screaming into overtime to decide ties. The fact that they still felt it necessary to award a point to the team that loses in overtime tells you how hard it was to give up on the idea. The point for losing in OT needs to go. So does the entire stupid point system. The shootout made it possible to eliminate ties altogether. Now there is always a winner and a loser. So what do you say we just go with Ws and Ls? You know, wins and losses, the way every other sport does it. No more point totals on the standings page, just games behind.

COLLEGE FOOTBALL

FORGET THE POLLS

No more voting for champions. The media should have stopped participating in this stupidity a long time ago. Journalists are not supposed to be a part of the story. They should have no say in who plays for the "championship." Coaches should refuse to vote, too.

You can't have a poll if nobody votes. So let's boycott the polls. Nobody votes. If the NCAA wants to let a computer pick its major football champion, fine.

So that means throwing out the playoff suggestions that include picking the top eight teams in the polls for a playoff. No voters, no voting. Let it be a tournament that includes conference champions and maybe a wild card or two. Maybe one year, the MAC would be up against the SEC in the first round. So what if it's a mismatch? It happens in the basketball tournament every year.

It's not that tough.

By having it be all about winning your conference, there would be no need for the top teams to schedule rent-a-victims to improve their rankings. An 8-4 record would be considered a rousing success if it meant a Big Ten Championship. Of course, this will never happen. Not when 105,000 show up for Ohio State and Akron.

COLLEGE STUDENTS ONLY

This is a really wild concept. If you can't get into my college as a student, you can't get in as a football or basketball player. No more stupid NCAA rules. Get back to college football and basketball being played by real college students. If the college presidents want to lower their standards to admit kids who read at the fourth grade level, let them.

COLLEGE BASKETBALL

CONTRACTION

Reduce the tournament from 66 to 32 teams or only invite teams whose chances of winning are better than their chances of being struck by lightning on the way to the arena. The 17 and 18 seeds are 4-204 since the tournament went from 32 to 66 teams.

Maybe you get a warm and fuzzy feeling watching Duke beat Hampton 87-45, I don't. Let Hampton play in its own tournament against teams that they might be able to beat.

SOCCER

Allow tackling. Reduce the writhing. Make it a federal crime to teach it to children. Not necessarily in that order.

YOUTH SPORTS

When did kids' sports get turned upside down? Was it when the divorce rates went up and mothers started getting involved?

Here's how it used to work: You learned, usually from your dad and/or older kids in the neighborhood, how to catch and throw a baseball. (Hitting was the last thing that you learned.)

When your parents were convinced that you liked baseball and had some idea how to play it, they looked into getting you into an organized youth league and on to a team.

In 2011, here's how it works: Parents decide that it's time for their kid to play baseball. Usually it's way before the kid actually knows anything about baseball or has any desire to play it — around six years old. Mom and dad find a league and get their kid on a team. They give him a uniform and take lots of pictures because he looks really cute. Then they put him on the field in his cute uniform and *pretend* that he's playing baseball. The parents and grandparents feel obligated to go to his games and they show up for every one of them with their folding chairs.

Nobody can catch.

Nobody can throw and nobody can hit.

The kids, when they're not batting, are standing around looking at birds, playing with the dirt and picking their noses. When the season is over, everybody gets a two-foot trophy. And America takes one more step toward total wussification.

Baseball is the hardest of the four major sports to learn, but I'm going to guess that it's still the one that most parents will sign their kid up for. It could be that soccer has surpassed baseball. If so, then total wussification may already be here.

The problem in baseball is the same in all sports. Kids are organized too soon.

The only thing that could get youth sports right-side up again is a willingness among parents to leave their kids alone and let them learn sports in the backyard and on the school playgrounds before they put them in uniforms. That's not going to happen because young mothers have come up with something called "play dates." The kids are dependent upon their mothers deciding when, what and with whom they play.

Their child's play time is part of their social time.

Once again, total wussification may have already arrived.

I can't imagine a childhood that was so dominated by my mother that she determined who I was going to play with on a daily basis.

And I wonder what's going to become of sports when all of these play-date kids grow up.

CHAPTER 19

QUOTES FROM THE UNFAMOUS

My friend Joe was one of the fastest runners ever to come out of the South Hills area – a WPIAL champion sprinter. He also started smoking when he was about 14 and was actually known to have smoked on his way to his track meets.

Eighteen or 20 years ago, when Joe was in his mid-forties, my wife and I were waiting outside a movie theater with him and his wife.

By this time, most of our friends had given up the habit. My wife Jeani asked Joe how long he had been smoking and he said, "Since I was about 14."

"Wow," Jeani said, "imagine what your lungs look like."

Joe's response:

"Who sees your lungs?"

That quote was widely circulated among my friends and a few years later my friend Pete was visiting Joe, who was in the hospital recovering from triple bypass surgery.

Pete said to Joe, "Now you know who sees your lungs — the guy who cracked open your sternum on his way to your heart."

Joe no longer smokes.

CHAPTER 20

I WISH I HAD KNOWN

actually thought about making the title of this book "I Wish I Had Known That I Was Going to Write This Book." I never dreamed that I would ever write a book and here I am writing my second one. If I had known, I would have taken notes every day and had a tape recorder rolling a lot more often.

A perfect example is the day in 1974 that I spent driving Satchel Paige, one of baseball's most legendary characters, around to media appearances in Wichita, Kan.

There's a chapter in my first book "Just Watch the Game" called "Satch" and it's about a page and a half long because I didn't know that I would be writing about that day 37 years in the future. I can only imagine the great material I could have had if I had put a tape recorder on the front seat of the car that day.

There are countless other examples of memorable meetings and experiences that would have been chapters that wrote themselves if I had been smart enough to make note of them at the time.

I've carried a ton of these stories in my head, but I never thought that they would end up in a book. None of them are worthy of a full chapter, but they're worth repeating. At least I think they are, but I guess you'll be the judge of that, won't you?

BOWMAN AFTER MIDNIGHT

In May of 1992 the Penguins were playing the Rangers in New York in the Patrick Division Finals. That series is remembered mostly for the slash by the Rangers' Adam Graves that broke Mario Lemieux's wrist.

When that happened, the Penguins weren't given much chance to win the series, but they ended up winning it and going on to win the Stanley Cup. The coach that year was Scottie Bowman. If there is a more successful coach in North American professional sports history, I don't know who he is.

He won nine Stanley Cups with three different teams. That's insane.

Bowman reminded me a lot of Chuck Noll. He didn't come across as the most friendly guy in the world, but he wasn't nearly as grouchy and serious as he seemed to be.

I loved covering those two Stanley Cup runs by the Penguins. I enjoyed them more than anything else that I did in my 30 years in television. I especially liked the road games because I was able to get a feel for how intense those playoff series can be and get an appreciation for what it's like for an NHL team to be in enemy territory.

It wasn't just about covering the games. It was also about being part of a major traveling party for six weeks and having breakfast and dinner and hanging out every day and night with all the media who were on the same beat.

Cindy Himes, who was the Penguins Media Relations Director, tried to be as accommodating as possible and she was aware of the long days that we all were putting in, so she arranged to have some food set out for us in one of the hotel meeting rooms. We were staying in the same hotel as the team.

Stan Savran (WTAE) and Sam Nover (WPXI) were on the same schedule that I was on. We all started early in the morning and finished at midnight after we did our 11 o'clock live shots back to Pittsburgh, so it was usually around 1 a.m. when we would get back to the hotel.

One night (and I think Stan and Sam were both there) a bunch of us media schlubs were scarfing the free food in the meeting room when Bowman walked in.

This was no small deal.

Chuck Tanner walking into a room full of media guys would not have been such a big deal because he was not nearly as standoffish with us as Bowman was. But at least in my experience, I had never looked at Bowman as a guy who had much interest in hanging with the media.

But here he was, Scotty Friggin' Bowman, taking a seat at the head of the table. It was at least one o'clock in the morning and he held court for at least an hour and told stories and passed on invaluable insights into the game of hockey.

And then we went to bed.

I don't remember one thing he said. I wish I had known I was going to write this book.

FIRST (AND LAST?) STEAK DINNER

In 1989 I came up with a brilliant idea for the February sweeps. The sweeps are when TV news directors are looking for highly promotable stories to be used to pump up viewership numbers when the ratings are measured. I suggested doing a story on Winter Baseball.

Ever since my days in the minor leagues and hearing players telling stories about their experiences in Venezuela, Puerto Rico and the Dominican Republic, I wanted to see it for myself.

The news director at KDKA, Sue McInerney, was all for it. If anybody suggested such a thing today he would be told to report to HR to find out about the company counseling program.

Producer Frank Wilson, cameraman Michael Challik and I were soon off to the Dominican Republic. We had arranged with the Pirates to have one of their scouts, Pablo Cruz, act as our guide. Pablo was a super nice guy and spoke English very well.

We stayed at a resort hotel/casino in Santo Domingo and Pablo warned us to watch out for the natives, who loved to prey on American tourists by selling them bogus jewelry and clothes and pulling other con games.

On our first day there, we met two 14-year-old kids, Ramon and Carlos, who wanted to know if they could earn a buck or two by carrying our equipment. I had brushed up on my high school and college Spanish before I left and was pretty proud of myself for being able to carry on a primitive conversation with them and they seemed like good kids to me.

We gave them a buck or two and they helped Michael carry the lights and the tripod. They were thrilled to be making a couple of bucks and Michael was glad to have them.

When Pablo saw them, he called them over and, even though it was in Spanish, it was easy to tell that the conversation wasn't very friendly and he was telling them to leave us alone.

Ramon and Carlos looked sad and I told Pablo that we would give them a shot and watch them carefully. He said something about keeping an eye on our wallets and said OK.

Ramon and Carlos came with us when we did some baseball-related stories on the island and we brought them back to the hotel when we were done for the day.

Frank, Michael and I were headed in the front door when I noticed the hotel doorman giving Ramon and Carlos the eye and the "What the hell are you doing here?" look. Then he gave them the universal "get outta here" gesture. You know, the flicking of the fingers like he's knocking ants off the picnic table.

That annoyed me, so I said, "They're with us." The doorman got an unhappy, skeptical look on his face and gestured for the boys to come through the doors and into the lobby. I'm pretty sure that it was the first time that either Ramon or Carlos had ever been allowed to set foot in a hotel lobby.

Keep in mind that the Dominican Republic is a poor country and I don't mean poor the way people in America think of poor. In the Dominican "poor" people don't own a car or a TV and they don't have air-conditioning.

(On our last day on the island, we were near the airport killing a few hours before catching our return flight and a bunch of kids were hanging around hoping to scrounge a dollar or two from us. None of them was wearing shoes. "Donde estan sus zapatos?" I asked in my primitive Spanish, which I was pretty sure meant, "Where are your shoes?" They all said that they didn't have any and when I asked "Nunca?" (Never?), they all said, "Si.")

So back to the hotel lobby. It's obvious that Carlos and Ramon are in disbelief and awe. They can't believe they're actually hanging around a hotel lobby with rich Americans.

I ask them if they're hungry.

"Si."

I told them to follow me to the restaurant. (They were each wearing their only pair of shoes, by the way.) As we're leaving the lobby I notice that both kids are looking over their shoulder at the doorman with the universal expression of "What are you gonna do about it?" look. The doorman was obviously pissed that riffraff had been allowed to get past him.

The look on the kids' faces when we all sat down at a table in the restaurant is something I'll never forget. They were completely stunned.

I handed each of them a menu and said, "Order whatever you want." They both looked at me sheepishly as if they didn't believe me. They saw the prices and couldn't believe I was serious.

I said it again. "Order whatever you want." They both ordered the best steak on the menu.

It was one of the most enjoyable, entertaining meals of my life. I just watched those kids enjoy the steaks. They kept looking at each other with "Can you believe this shit?" looks and the more they ate the more I enjoyed it.

I told them to order desert.

At some point I asked them how long it had been since they had eaten a steak. They said, "Nunca." In case you weren't paying attention earlier, that's never. Before that day they had never eaten in a restaurant, much less eaten a steak.

From that point on I never worried about Carlos and Ramon ripping us off.

Before you give me too much credit, keep in mind that I was on an expense account and that dinner went on the KDKA ledger as a "production meeting." But I would have paid twice what I paid to see the expression on the faces of those two kids when the waiter plopped those steaks in front of them.

They worked for us every day while we were there and were a big help. The dinner was well worth it in more ways than one.

Ramon had become especially fascinated with my Sony Watchman. Remember those handheld, black-and-white TVs with the one-inch screen? It cost about $125 and I liked having it with me to kill time in airports. I let Ramon take it home with him one night and he told me that his entire family watched a Winter League baseball game on it.

They, of course, couldn't imagine owning a TV. On the last day, I gave it to him to keep. For a long time after that I had a picture in my mind of a large family gathered around a TV with a one-inch screen and thinking they had struck it rich.

That trip forever changed the meaning of the word "poor" for me.

LUNCH WITH THE PROFESSOR

Sometime in the late '80s I went to Oakland, California, to cover a flag football game between the Steelers and Raiders of the '70s.

I don't know how, but I ended up in a bar, sitting at a table eating lunch with a bunch of former Raiders including Ben Davidson. None of them knew who I was or why I was there and neither did I.

As I sat down, these players that I had never met introduced me to another non-Raider who was dining with us.

It was Professor Irwin Corey.

I guess you have to be of a certain age to know who he is and why it would be so weird to be sitting across from him at lunch.

He was a comedian who had Einstein-like hair and wore black-and-white sneakers with an oversized, disheveled sports jacket and spoke in doubletalk. He had been a pretty big deal at one time and was a regular on "The Tonight Show" and other variety shows. He came across as completely insane. Here are a couple of his quotes:

"I want do die in my sleep like my grandfather … Not screaming and yelling like the passengers in his car."

"Oh, you hate your job? Why didn't you say so? There's a support group for that. It's called *everybody*, and they meet at the bar."

"When I was a kid, I prayed to the Lord for a new bicycle. Then I realized that the Lord doesn't work that way. So, I stole a bike and asked the Lord to forgive me."

I had seen him a thousand times on television and here I was trying to make lunch-table small talk with Professor Irwin Corey. I don't remember anything he said, but I remember being thoroughly entertained. If I had known I was writing this book, I'm sure I'd have more for you.

O.J.

I was walking through the Steelers' office at Three Rivers Stadium one day in the late-'80s. As I walked past Art Rooney's former office, which had been turned into a sort of mini-museum, I noticed a guy in there looking through some of the memorabilia. When he looked up I saw that it was O.J. Simpson, whom I had never met.

I nodded at him and he said, "Hi, John."

I said "Hi" and kept going.

To this day, I don't know why he would have known my name.

Do you think if I passed by his prison cell in Nevada he'd say, "Hi, John?"

FUMBLING ON JOEPA

In 1973, I was working at my first job at little Color Channel 3 in Sharon, Pa. It was a small, local cable-TV station that was way ahead of its time. We did a local 6 and 11 o'clock newscast six days a week, covering the news and sports of the Shenango Valley.

One of my first big interviews was with Penn State coach Joe Paterno, who, believe it or not, was still a relatively young college football coach. (Boy, am I old.)

He was appearing in town at a banquet and probably trying to recruit Sharon High's stud defensive end Randy Holloway, who would eventually go to Pitt and become an All American and the Minnesota Vikings' Number One draft pick.

When I was starting out, I was terrified of interviews. I thought I would be intimidated by famous people and I worried that I would run out of questions.

I was pretty nervous all day thinking about my one-on-one sit down with Paterno. But I introduced myself and he was very nice and actually acted like he was interested in being interviewed by something called Color Channel 3.

I took my little plastic microphone and looked to the cameraman standing behind the black-and-white Porta-Pak camera and he tells me the tape is rolling and I ask my first brilliant question. And as I move the tiny plastic mic toward Paterno's face for his response, I fumble.

The mic comes tumbling out of my hand and lands in Joe's lap. He had to pick it up and give it to me so we could start over.

I wanted to run out of the room and hurl myself in front of a really large truck, but Paterno was nice about it and the rest of the interview went off without a hitch.

As I headed back to the station I was beating myself up for my major gaffe when I got an idea. It was an early sign of my willingness to come across as a smart shit on the air. Instead of dwelling on my embarrassment, which no one would ever have seen, I decided to use the portion of the tape where I fumbled and to make fun of myself.

I set it up by saying what a big deal it was to interview Joe Paterno and then I showed my "fumble" several times in slow motion. I analyzed why I thought the fumble occurred and actually turned it into a pretty funny bit.

Amazingly enough, here I am 38 years later and that is still the only fumble of my career.

MAZ WHO?

If you're a sports fan, especially if you're a Pittsburgh sports fan, you would probably love to play a round of golf with Bill Mazeroski.

In the late '80s, I played in a fivesome with Maz in a charity golf tournament at South Hills Country Club. We had just hit our tee shots on our first hole and still hadn't seen the fifth member of our scramble team.

I was in a golf cart pulling out and I remember thinking what a shame it was that somebody missed out on a chance to play golf with the guy who hit the most famous home run in history.

Just then, a guy came running up to the tee with his driver in his hand. We waited and he hit his tee ball. Then he jumped into my cart, apologized profusely for any inconvenience and said, "Who's our celebrity?"

I told him who it was and he said, "Really, what sport did he play? Was it baseball? I think somebody said he hit an important home run or something?"

I told him about the 1960 home run and he wasn't the least bit impressed.

If my memory is correct, he was a brain surgeon.

MICK THE PRICK

One night in the Summer of 1976 my wife Jeani asked me, "Who's Mickey Mantle?" That should give you an idea of how much my wife of almost 40 years knows and cares about sports.

She knew that Mantle was a big deal because the night that she asked the question was "Mickey Mantle Night" at Watt Powell Park in Charleston, W.Va. That's where the Pirates AAA affiliate was located and I was doing the radio play-by-play. Jeani had a job working in the ticket booth.

Earlier in the day I had had my first and only encounter with Mantle.

I had to call him at his hotel room to do an interview for the pre-game show. I called and it went something like this:

"Hello."

"Hi, Mickey. I'm the radio play-by-play voice for the Charlies and I was wondering …."

"What time is it?"

(I don't remember exactly what time it was but it was late morning.)

"OK. When do you want to do this?

"Now, if that's OK."

It wasn't one of the better interviews I had ever done. Mantle had no patience and gave me short, boring answers.

Looking back on it, it's hard to blame him.

We're talking about Mickey Mantle here. He's in Charleston Friggin' West Virginia, reduced to taking swings against AAA pitchers and then getting into his car and heading for the next team willing to pay him $1,000.

Mickey Mantle swinging at batting practice lobs is about as depressing as it gets, especially when he can't hit one out of the infield, which he didn't.

After Jeani closed her ticket window, she walked by the area where Mantle had just finished signing autographs. A nice, little old man came up to Mantle with a souvenir bat. He told Mantle that it had already been signed by Lou Gehrig and Lefty Gomez. Mantle snapped, "I don't care who signed it. Signing time is over. I'm done."

He actually blew the guy off.

Mantle did a good job of rehabilitating his image in the last year or two of his life and did a lot of apologizing and explaining.

It didn't work with my wife.

MONEY FOR NOTHING

I've been asked to star in two movies.

OK, I wasn't asked to star in them. I was asked to be an extra.

In "Just Watch the Game" I wrote about my experiences with Ron Howard in "Gung Ho," starring Michael Keaton. I was in the movie for about 12 seconds, but actually received a compliment from Howard for my searing portrayal of a guy pushing a shopping cart in a supermarket.

In late 1992 or early 1993, I got a call from local Pittsburgh casting director Donna Belajac. The producers of a movie being shot in Pittsburgh called "Money For Nothing" and starring John Cusack had seen me on KDKA and decided that I would be perfect to play the role of a news reporter.

Not a sports guy. A news guy.

I thought it over for about four seconds and accepted the offer.

We never got around to discussing salary.

The movie was based on the true story of an unemployed dockworker named Joey Doyle (Cusack) who found $1.2 million that had fallen off an armored truck.

I got a good lesson in why movies cost so much to make.

After I agreed to play the part, I was told to report to the Westin William Penn Hotel a few weeks later to work with the wardrobe department.

When I got there I was asked which part I was playing and the staff began handing me different articles of clothing. Pants, shirt, jacket (my scene would be shot outside in cold weather), right down to the belt and, believe it or not, the socks.

I started wondering if I was going to be shooting a striptease scene. They didn't pick any underwear out for me. This went on for quite a while with quite a bit of discussion about which belt looked better.

Keep in mind that in my scene I played a reporter in a large group of media waiting outside of a police station.

The owner of the truck company has just found out that the money fell off the truck and as he's coming into the police station I stick a microphone in his face and say, "Do you think your insurance will cover it?"

That's it. That was my part.

They never took a close-up of my socks.

They actually gave me a trailer.

On the day that I was scheduled to shoot my scene, I reported to the location somewhere in Lawrenceville. They told me that I could wait in my trailer. I was expecting a living room, a kitchen, a bathroom and maybe two bedrooms.

It was a trailer. As in tractor-trailer truck.

The door had my name on it and when I went inside, I found that I had barely enough room to sit, so I decided to head for the building that was being used as the police station. That's where most of the extras were hanging out waiting for their scene. I sat there for at least six hours.

Finally, someone came to get me and the other people who were going to be playing media schlubs in the scene. I felt a little superior to them since I knew that I was the one with the speaking part. I actually thought they could have done a better job of treating me in a way that my star status deserved, but I bit the bullet and headed for the front of the building.

We did several takes and I got my line right every time.

That took another two or three hours. So it amounted to at least a 10-hour day for my 10-second scene. I felt good about my performance and thought that it was only a matter of time before I was called to do more meatier roles.

Maybe do a nude scene. Nothing gratuitous, of course.

The scene never made it into the movie.

I ended up on the cutting room floor.

THE CALLED SHOT

One of my most memorable interviews was also one of my first. In 1974, I was at Cubs spring training in Scottsdale, Arizona. As the new voice of the Cubs AAA affiliate in Wichita, Kansas, the purpose of my trip was to meet the Aeros' manager and coaches and get acquainted with the players. I also was hoping to get lots of interviews in the can to use in my early-season pregame shows.

Charlie Grimm was a roving instructor for the Cubs and a former player and manager. He was 76 at the time and had been around baseball for over 50 years. I'm sure he knew a nervous, confused rookie when he saw one and he couldn't have been nicer to me when I approached him for an interview. I found out firsthand why they called him "Jolly Cholly."

When someone told me that Grimm was playing first base for the Cubs in Babe Ruth's famous "Called Shot" game, I couldn't believe it.

I had only been on the job for a week or two and I was still pinching myself a lot to see if I was dreaming. I loved baseball and I couldn't believe that I was now being paid to do nothing but watch and talk about what was, by far, my favorite sport. And here I was with a chance to talk to a guy who played against Babe Ruth.

If I had known I was writing this book, I would have saved the taped interview that I did with him. Over the years, I've heard lots of versions of what actually happened in World Series Game 3 in 1932.

The film shows that Ruth definitely gestured toward centerfield and Ruth always said that he was pointing to the flagpole and saying that he was going to hit the next pitch out there.

Some other oldtimers said that he was pointing toward the Cubs dugout and some said he was holding up two fingers to tell the Cubs players who were heckling him that it was only two strikes.

Charlie said (and he said it with conviction) that Ruth wasn't pointing to centerfield. He said he was pointing to the mound.

According to Charlie, Guy Bush, the next day's starting pitcher for the Cubs, was one of the loudest hecklers in the Cubs dugout during that at bat and Ruth was talking to him when he gestured toward the mound. Charlie said "The Babe (he always referred to him as "The Babe") pointed to the mound and said, 'Bush, watch what you say, you're gonna be out there tomorrow.' "

Ruth hit the next pitch into the centerfield seats.

Charlie said that when the called-shot stuff started, all the players just went along with it because they thought it made a great story and it was good for the game.

For the next couple of days, every once in a while, I would stop and shake my head in disbelief. I couldn't get over the fact that I had spoken to a guy who had played against Babe Ruth and been on the field for one of the most famous moments in baseball history.

By the way, Guy Bush lasted a third of an inning in Game 4.

COFFEY'S CUP

The press boxes at Three Rivers Stadium and Pitt Stadium had one bathroom and I don't think either of them was marked "Men."

There was no need to designate them because, when those buildings were built, there were no women in the press box.

I was a working member of the media when women started showing up to cover sports and I was working when it was decreed by Major League Baseball that women were to be allowed in the locker room.

That seems like nothing now, but it was a huge deal then.

If I had known I was going to write this book, I know I would have paid a lot closer attention to the details of what happened the first night that women went into the Pirates locker room.

There were only two women covering the Pirates at the time, but I remember a lot more showing up that night, including a local female TV reporter or two.

I don't remember all the details, but I think there were several players in the locker room who played with themselves a lot. The women who ventured in did their best to keep their eyes at chest level, but they had to have gotten an eyeful.

I know women like to say, "If you've seen one, you've seen them all," but those are not women who have been in professional sports locker rooms.

In the early days of women in the locker room, the players did very little to adjust. Most of them weren't shy at all about coming out of the shower and walking across the entire room naked.

As the years went by and more and more women showed up, they started covering up more. The ladies would never admit it, but there have always been and probably still are more than a few crotch watchers.

The most blatant I ever saw was in 1991, during the Penguins' run to the Stanley Cup. There was a woman working for a national radio network walking around with a tape recorder and she made no effort to hide the fact that she was interested in looking at naked men.

She covered the team throughout the playoffs, home and away, and about halfway through the run everybody in the media and all the Penguins players knew what she was up to.

This woman would enter the locker room after a practice or a game and head right for a spot near the showers. The other women who were covering the series would make a point to always have their backs to the area where the players came out of the shower.

This chick planted herself there by the showers and gazed at the door waiting for naked players to emerge. The players had more important things to worry about, but it started to get on their nerves.

Finally, after a game in Minnesota, Paul Coffey apparently had had enough. He came out of the locker room naked, carrying his dirty laundry bag, gave the woman a look and threw the bag at her feet and walked away.

The series ended shortly after that and I never saw the woman again. Maybe she became a urologist.

CHAPTER 21

PITTSBURGH'S BADDEST MAN EVER

Forget Jack Lambert.

Forget Joe Greene.

Forget James Harrison.

Forget Billy Conn.

The baddest man ever to live and/or work in Pittsburgh is a guy you have probably never heard of.

He was only a little over six feet tall and weighed about 180 pounds. If you grew up in Western Pennsylvania, you should have heard of him. In fact, there should be a large statue of this guy standing right next to the fountain in Point State Park.

If you've never heard of Sam Brady, it's probably not your fault.

It's your history teacher's fault.

Since you're reading this book, I think it's safe to assume that you have heard of Jim Kelly. He's a Hall of Fame quarterback who played for the Buffalo Bills in the '80s and '90s. And he's from East Brady, Pa.

East Brady as in Sam Brady.

You've probably heard of Brady's Bend and you may be aware of Brady's Run State Park and Brady's Lake. But I'll bet your history teacher never told you about this guy who had so many places named after him.

• • •

Sam Brady was to Pennsylvania, Ohio and West Virginia what Daniel Boone was to Kentucky.

Captain Sam Brady, whose beard obviously influenced the Steelers' Brett Keisel.

And he was one tough son of a bitch.

This is a guy who, while walking with his friend, was confronted by a large black bear. Both he and his friend had left their rifles back at the cabin. His friend turned and ran for the cabin. Sam took out his tomahawk, charged the bear and took him out with one chop to the head.

Unlike, say, James Harrison, Brady wasn't wearing a helmet, face mask and shoulder pads. And the bear saw him coming. That was no cheap shot.

I've always been interested in history and late in life I discovered that my history teachers dropped the ball when it came to making me aware of just how rich in history Western Pennsylvania is.

About 15 years ago I was reading a book called "Undaunted Courage" by Stephen Ambrose. It's about the Lewis and Clark expedition. I know that we were taught about Lewis and Clark's trip out West in the early 1800s, but I was shocked to find out early in the book that Meriwether Lewis had his keelboat built in Pittsburgh. He had to spend a couple of extra weeks here waiting for it because the builder had a drinking problem and was way behind schedule.

Maybe I wasn't paying attention — something I excelled at in school — when they told us that Lewis started the expedition by putting the boat in the water not too far from where the Golden Triangle is now, but I think I would have remembered.

Every school kid in America is taught (or at least used to be taught) about the Lewis and Clark Expedition, but only the school kids in Western Pennsylvania could claim that it started in their neighborhood.

I think maybe Pittsburgh's connection to Lewis and Clark should have been emphasized more in our history classes. But that wasn't the only case of my history teachers missing the boat, as I learned just a few years ago.

I went to Our Lady of Grace School in Scott Township from the fifth through the eighth grade. It's located on Bower Hill Road.

In my lifetime, I have probably spent more time riding up and down Bower Hill Road than any road on the planet. When I waited for the Bigi Bus downtown in the late 1950s, I looked for the one that said "Bower Hill" on the front.

It wasn't until a few years ago that I became aware of the Battle of Bower Hill.

The battle took place outside the window of the room where I was learning American history from Mr. Miller.

You would think that a teacher would use that little piece of history to get the attention of a classroom full of 13-year-olds who were constantly complaining about how boring and useless history class was.

I'll bet Mr. Miller never heard of the Battle of Bower Hill.

In the 1790s, less than 100 yards away from Our Lady of Grace School and within a few feet of Our Lady of Grace Church, General John Neville lived in the biggest mansion west of the Allegheny Mountains.

He had been awarded 1,000 acres in 1774 for having fought in Lord

Dunmore's War. (I would take part in my first football practice in an apple grove that was located on the spot where the church was soon to be built. I wonder if those trees were planted by John Neville.)

In 1791 Congress passed a federal excise tax on whiskey and George Washington chose Neville to collect the revenue. You've probably heard of the Whiskey Rebellion. Neville, who fought with Washington and spent a winter at Valley Forge with him, was opposed to the tax at first, but later agreed to collect the taxes and the locals thought he had been bribed.

Neville turned out to be the only tax collector in the country who tried to enforce the law. The guys he hired to help him collect the taxes were tarred and feathered and he feared for his own safety, so he asked Washington for help.

Farmers were being dragged all the way to Philadelphia to face charges of refusing to pay the taxes.

On July 16, 1794, about 500 men, led by Oliver Miller and James McFarlane, showed up in Neville's front yard and demanded that he resign. Neville sent out his armed slaves and the soldiers that had been sent by Washington. (I think Mr. Miller also would have gotten my attention if he had told me that slaves had lived on the playground where we played games of "Kill the Man.")

When the battle was over Oliver Miller and James McFarlane were dead and Neville's mansion was burned to the ground. The battle sent the message that the people of Southwest Pennsylvania were serious about not wanting to have their whiskey taxed. There was even talk of secession. Eventually the rebellion died down and Neville kept his job and stayed in the Bower Hill area.

I think that's a pretty interesting story and I think I would have found it interesting as a sixth or seventh grader. I wonder how many of the thousands of kids who have gone through Our Lady of Grace School are aware of all the history that was outside their window during history class.

• • •

It's not surprising that very few Pittsburghers and Southwest Pennsylvanians are aware of Sam Brady, Pittsburgh's "Baddest Man Ever." Because he was an Indian fighter, present-day political correctness will probably prevent him from making an appearance in local history classes any time soon. But when he was living in this neighborhood in the late 18th and early 19th centuries, Brady's neighbors were happy to have him around to hunt and kill Indians.

Indians were constantly trying to kill them.

Sam Brady left his parents farm in Shippensburg at 19 to join the Revolutionary War in 1775. He fought in several battles in the Boston area and eventually fought with George Washington. He crossed the Delaware with him in 1776.

Because of his demonstrations of bravery and leadership, Brady was a lieutenant by the time he was 20. At the battle of Paoli, he was trying to get away from some redcoats when one of them pinned him to a fence by sticking a bayonet through his coat. Brady ripped himself free and then killed a cavalryman who had caught up with him.

During the war, Brady paid a visit to his family's farm in Shippensburg and found his brother had been mutilated and killed by Indians.

That really pissed him off and he vowed to dedicate his life to killing Indians. That may sound a little harsh in 2011, but guys dedicated to killing Indians were good to have around when your neighbors were being butchered in their fields and in their homes.

Sometime around 1778, the British were paying Indians to harass the settlers who lived in the vicinity of Fort Pitt. Brady was sent there and told to recruit the best fighters in the area and put together a special force to hunt down and kill Indians.

They became known as "Brady's Rangers."

Sort of like "Franco's Italian Army" or "Lambert's Lunatics," only a little more dangerous and a lot more serious.

These guys became America's first special forces.

Brady started by drafting seven men, all great athletes who were great hand-to-hand fighters and marksmen. They could paddle a mean canoe and had really good times in the 40.
 Brady was the absolute leader and his orders had to be followed without question. Nobody fired a shot until he said so. They dressed in buckskin leggings and shirts and moccasins. Some of them followed Brady's lead and wore a black do-rag. They wore war paint (kind of like eye-black) and had their own set of hand signals.

It didn't take long for Brady to develop a reputation for toughness and ruthlessness among the Indians. Kind of like James Harrison in the AFC. The difference, of course, was that while Harrison's actions may have caused him to be penalized, fined and/or suspended, Brady's actions, if he were caught, would have caused him to be burned at the stake.

Very slowly.

Keeping that in mind when you hear some of the things this wild man did will give you an idea of just how much of a badass he was. Every time he suited up to play, he knew that if he lost it would mean being tortured and burned. So it took a pretty large set of balls for him and two other rangers to agree to spy on the Indians in a settlement in Ohio called Sandusky Towns.

On the way back, they were discovered and chased by Indians. They lost all of their food and their gunpowder had gotten wet because they had to cross several streams. They only had one ball (bullet) left — the one in Brady's musket.

Brady left the other two rangers and went off to see if he could kill some food with his one shot. Not long after he left them, Brady came upon five Wyandot warriors, four of them walking, one on horseback. There was a young white boy tied to the Indian who was on horseback and a white woman was following behind, tethered to the horse.

Brady recognized the woman as Jane Stupes, whom he knew had been kidnapped a few days earlier from her settlement on Chartiers Creek near what is now Bridgeville. He could have stayed quiet and let them pass, but if he had you wouldn't be reading about it now.

Brady used his one shot to put a hole in the forehead of the Indian on horseback. Then he yelled out, "Come on, get 'em boys," hoping that the other four Indians would think they were under attack.

It was the 1792 version of disguising the blitz.

The other four Indians scattered. Brady tried to untie the boy but couldn't. He grabbed Jane Stupes by the hand and started to run. She was confused at first because Brady was dressed as an Indian, but she was OK after Brady identified himself. They outran the other Indians and were able to lose them. Brady eventually borrowed a canoe in Beaver and took Jane up the Ohio River to safety at Fort Pitt. Her son would turn up several years later in a prisoner exchange.

You've heard of NFL players having their vertical leap measured. Sam Brady made one of the most famous horizontal leaps in American history.

He had been chasing a group of Indians into what is now known as Portage County, Ohio, and he ambushed them near a small lake. (If you've driven on I-80 to go to Cleveland for a Steelers-Browns game, you've passed it many times. It's called Brady's Lake.) A second group of Indians came along and captured Brady and his men.

Remember, he knew that he was a prize catch and that if he were caught he would die a slow, agonizing death.

The Indians knew exactly who he was and they planned their version of a major tailgate party. He was going to be burned at the stake, but Brady was such a big deal that they kept him confined so that they could invite the surrounding tribes to the party, including, of course, the Cleveland Indians, led by Chief Wahoo, who was such a big fan of burnings at the stake that seeing one would cause him to walk around with a perpetual stupid grin on his face.

Brady was stripped naked and made to run the gauntlet.

A good 40 time came in handy if you were ever chosen for that lovely exercise. Every Indian in the village formed two lines and you had to run the length of the line while they clubbed, stabbed or poked you with whatever they chose. (The 18th century version of covering a kickoff.) The only rule was that they had to hit you from behind after you went by. They didn't want you falling down and ruining the effect.

After he ran the gauntlet, Brady was tied to a stake. Not the way you've seen it in the movies. The Indians liked to tie your hands and then tether you to a tree so that you were free to run and hop on the burning coals.

They thought that was really entertaining.

Brady was a pretty strong guy and somehow, maybe with the help of the fire's heat, he was able to break through the rope. He grabbed a squaw who was holding a baby and threw both of them into the fire. That distracted the other Indians and he sprinted for the woods.

He had no clothes, no food and no weapons.

After several days and probably a hundred miles of running (and the Steelers think their run test at St. Vincent College is tough), Brady was hoping to cross the Cuyahoga River (the one that caught on fire in Cleveland in the '70s) at a well-known crossing spot, but the Indians were waiting for him there.

So Brady headed for another spot upstream. He came to an area that was about 25 feet above the water, which was a roaring current. It was between 20 and 25 feet to the other side and the Indians were in hot pursuit.

Brady did the only thing he could do. He backed up, took a running start and jumped. He landed a few feet below the top of the other bank and scrambled to the top.

(The spot, near Kent, Ohio, is marked "Brady's Leap" by a monument that says the distance from one side of the river to the other was 23 feet. This makes Jack Lambert the second baddest man ever to come through Kent.)

The Indians were stunned and had no intention of attempting the same leap. They started shooting at Brady and hit him in the leg. The Indians eventually found another place to cross and continued their pursuit. So, now, Brady is still naked, he has been running for 100 miles and he has a hole in one of his legs.

Did I mention he was tough?

He eventually eluded the Indians by jumping into what is now Brady Lake and hiding under the water while breathing through a hollow reed. Eventually, despite not having any money for turnpike tolls, Brady somehow made it back to Fort Pitt.

A few years later, Brady was charged by the state of Pennsylvania with unjustifiably killing two Indians. By this time, Brady was a bigger deal in Pittsburgh than Ben Roethlisberger could ever hope to be and hundreds of people, many of them armed, were gathered outside the courtroom in Market Square, ready to spring him if he was found guilty.

Brady was found not guilty and was cheered from both banks of the Monongahela River when he boarded a boat with his wife and kids and headed home. Brady lived out his life with his wife Drusilla and his children until he died at the ripe old age of 37. He's buried in West Liberty, West Virginia.

Why this guy's name isn't known to every kid who grew up in Western Pennsylvania, I'll never know.

Sam Brady was a Revolutionary War hero who crossed the Delaware with George Washington. That alone should have gotten him a lot more ink and lot more time devoted to him in our local history classes.

Pittsburgh's and Western Pennsylvania's early settlers owed their lives to this guy who risked a hideous death every time he went to work.

A huge statue of him paddling a canoe would be fitting and would be a pretty impressive sight sitting on The Point in the Golden Triangle. At the very least, "The Baddest Man in Pittsburgh History" deserves a spot at Pittsburgh International Airport next to Franco Harris.

CHAPTER 22

SHORT STOP

PUKE LIKE A CHAMPION TODAY

Every football fan should make at least one pilgrimage to South Bend, Indiana, for a Notre Dame football game. It doesn't matter if you're a Notre Dame lover, a Notre Dame hater or if you're neither.

And it is a pilgrimage.

The campus and the stadium reek of history and tradition. Notre Dame football (and college football, for that matter) may not be what it used to be, but it's still the college football team that they make movies about.

I made my first trip out to South Bend for a Pitt game in 1986 and I followed the advice of people who had been there many times and made sure that I arrived on campus early in the morning on game day.

It was a perfect, crisp, cool, sunny fall Saturday with plenty of colorful leaves left on the trees. I walked around the campus by myself and took it all in. I think I actually did hear some echoes.

Everybody told me I should check out the campus bookstore a couple of hours before the game and I did that, too. Lots of people buying lots of Notre Dame stuff.

As I walked around the campus with the thousands of fans who were enjoying the same scene that I was, I kept thinking that it was almost too perfect to be true. And I hadn't even gotten to the stadium yet.

I had seen the stadium up close and empty the day before when I went there for Pitt's walk-through practice. I heard a ton of echoes that day as I stood on the field surrounded by the empty seats and I have to admit to getting a little chill when I walked under the "Play Like a Champion Today" sign that Notre Dame's players see just before entering the field.

On game day I got to the press box early and enjoyed the scene for as long as I could. Looking out the back of the press box I was able to get a bird's-eye view of what looked like a too-good-to-be-true scene from a movie. I was told to make sure I got a good look at the Notre Dame band marching through campus.

Every few seconds I would be struck by what a perfect, surreal scene it was. Blue sky, crisp air, colored leaves and then the band. I watched as the Notre Dame band marched to the end-zone gate and noticed the murmur of the crowd.

Suddenly the gates flew open and the band came blasting through playing the Notre Dame fight song.

Again, too perfect to be true.

I stood in the press box drinking it all in and thinking, "Boy, am I glad I'm here." It was another one of those times when I realized how lucky I was to have the job that I had.

The fans were roaring and the band was playing the fight song and performing its routine on the field and then, in the middle of all that beauty, pageantry and perfection I saw one little flaw.

One of the guys wearing a kilt and carrying a baton stepped out of formation.

And then he puked.

And when I say puke, I'm talking about major spewing that was clearly visible from where I was, high above the field.

After the first spew, he got himself together and got back in formation, but I could see that he was wobbling like an early Mike Tyson opponent in an early round.

Again, in the middle of the beauty, pageantry and perfection, he stepped out and puked again. And, again, with some help from a guy who had been standing on the sideline, he got back in formation.

Now, I'm no longer focused on the crisp air, the blue sky and the Notre Dame fight song. I'm rooting — along with several other guys in the press box who also had picked him out of the pageantry — for him to make it through the routine. We were also laughing hysterically and hoping he would puke one more time.

He did.

And it was green.

Perfect.

CHAPTER 23

MOORER OR LESS

I always loved doing TV stories about boxing. The visuals were great and the characters were rich. The trainers worked for little or no money and had a pure love for their sport that I never found in any other sport. I loved talking to the oldtime fighters and trainers on and off camera and I was always looking for a good local boxing story.

One local story that I had missed in the early to mid-'80s was Michael Moorer, the kid from Monessen, Pa., who had a meteoric rise to the top of the national amateur rankings.

When he started knocking out every light heavyweight who got in his way after turning pro, I started paying more attention, but by then he had relocated to Detroit and the famous Kronk gym that had produced many great fighters, including former welterweight champion Thomas Hearns.

Moorer won the light heavyweight championship in his 12th pro fight and he eventually became one of the best light heavyweight champions of all time with nine successful title defenses. He also eventually came to realize that the big money was in the heavyweight division, where he wouldn't have to worry about his weight so much.

When he started knocking out every heavyweight they put in front of him, I decided it was time to turn Michael Moorer into a local story because I was convinced that he would soon be fighting for the Heavyweight Championship of the World.

Even though his family lived in Monessen and he visited there regularly, Moorer never seemed to be enthusiastic about presenting himself as another successful, famous Western Pennsylvania athlete.

But I decided he was from Monessen the same way that Joe Montana was from Monongahela and I decided to pitch KDKA news director Sue McInerney on the idea of spending a week in Vegas with Moorer as he prepared for a fight.

I also had to go into General Manager Joe Berwanger's office and sell him on the idea — something we almost never had to do. I told Berwanger this kid is going to fight for the heavyweight championship sometime in the next couple of years and I want to own the story.

The two other local TV stations and the papers were doing a good job of ignoring Moorer and I said this could be one time when we don't wait for the newspapers or a network to do a story before we jump all over it. Let them follow our lead for a change.

Keep in mind that there is no one in local news today who would embarrass himself by pitching a story like this to his news director. I was talking about me, a cameraman and a producer going to Las Vegas for eight days. In 2011, when local stations like KDKA are pinching every penny, if you can't drive there in a car, you probably shouldn't waste your time pitching the story.

Joe Berwanger said go and before long I was meeting Moorer as he got off a commercial flight in Las Vegas and following him through the airport with a cameraman and a producer.

Moorer was there in late January of 1992 to fight Mike White, another handpicked opponent who would help Moorer build his resume on the way to a title fight. Moorer was being trained by Emanuel Stewart at the time and fighting on the same card as some guy named Lennox Lewis.

It was my first time in Vegas but it was my second time covering a major fight. I had covered the Larry Holmes-Renaldo Snipes Heavyweight Championship fight in Pittsburgh in 1981 and that was one of the most enjoyable weeks of my career.

Moorer was fighting White at Caesar's Palace and we found out right away that we were going to be special guests at the hotel. The PR lady made it clear from the first day that we would have free tickets to front-row seats at any of the shows and full access to the fighters. This wasn't a fight card that was going to get the hotel a lot of publicity, but the PR lady wanted to make sure that everyone in Pittsburgh heard the name Caesar's Palace as often as possible.

We spent time every day at Moorer's training sessions and had full access to Stewart, one of the all-time great trainers. There were lots of other boxing characters to talk to on and off camera and I soaked it all up.

I remember the first time we went to the ballroom where Moorer was training. I had been there a few minutes earlier to watch Lennox Lewis workout and, as I was returning to the ballroom, I was struck by how loud the sound of the glove hitting the heavy bag was. When I walked into the room, I saw that it was Moorer punching the heavy bag and I was surprised by how much louder his punches sounded than Lewis'.

It reminded me of the story that Moorer's grandfather, Henry Smith, had told me a few days before we flew to Vegas. Smith was a boxing trainer in Monessen and he raised Michael. When Moorer was 10 or 11, Smith let him come to the gym with him. As Smith was off attending to one of his fighters, he heard loud sounds coming from the area where the heavy bag was hanging.

It was Michael.

Smith knew a natural when he saw one and that was the beginning of Moorer's life as a boxer. Smith would later sue Moorer and claim that he had signed a contract that gave him 25 percent of Moorer's earnings. He had become a nuisance to Moorer's new trainers and management people and was left behind when Michael made the big time.

Moorer was much more impressive in the gym than Lennox Lewis. There was a lot of discussion about the fact that Moorer was a southpaw, including Lewis' trainer telling me that southpaws should all be put on a large boat and thrown into the ocean. Trainers hate training their fighters for southpaws because they're such a rarity. There were good fighters who had no interest in fighting Moorer because of his left-handed stance.

Moorer's opponent, Mike "The Giant" White, was 6'-10".

Of course, the best fight would have been Moorer vs. Lewis, but that's not how boxing works. If you have title aspirations, you don't fight serious contenders and give boxing fans the best show possible. You fight tomato cans and journeymen. Two future heavyweight champs were staying in that hotel that week, but they wouldn't be facing each other.

Both Moorer and Lewis won unanimous decisions, with Lewis' win coming over Levi Billups. I brought back some great images and behind-the-scenes stories about two up-and-coming heavyweight fighters, one of them a local kid.

Or was he local?

That's when I discovered Moorer's reluctance to identify with Monessen and Western Pennsylvania. When he was introduced that night, ring announcer Michael Buffer said Moorer was from Detroit, Michigan. If I was going to get any more trips to Vegas to cover him, Moorer was going to have to do a better job of identifying with Western Pa.

I got the feeling that Moorer was reluctant to identify with his hometown because of the way he was treated when he went home.

Apparently, there were lots of people who felt that he owed them something and there were plenty of people who were happy to tell him that he would never become heavyweight champ.

Michael was never known to hold his liquor well and that created problems. I think he stayed away from Monessen because he knew he would get into trouble if he spent too much time there.

I thought it was a shame because I knew how much Pittsburgh and Western Pa. would have gotten behind him as he made his way toward a title fight. You saw what happened when Hines Ward was competing for a stupid dancing title. Imagine a local kid fighting for, winning and defending the heavyweight championship of the world.

Detroit couldn't have cared less.

After watching them both fight, I left Las Vegas thinking that Moorer would kick Lewis' ass. Moorer was a knockout machine. He had TKO'd Levi Billups in the third round six months earlier and the win over White made him 27-0 with 25 knockouts as a light heavyweight and a heavyweight. Eight more wins and six more knockouts and it was time to fight Evander Holyfield.

I was going to be ringside at the Moorer-Holyfield fight to see what I always considered a local kid fighting for the Heavyweight Championship of the World. For me, especially after getting to know Moorer, it was as big as any World Series, Super Bowl or Stanley Cup Final.

The access that the media had to the two fighters in Vegas was amazing. The day before the fight I was hanging in Holyfield's hotel room with 10 or 12 other media guys, some from the UK, Japan and South America. It was more conversation than news conference.

Moorer's handlers still hadn't come around to accentuating Moorer's Western Pa. roots, but he was getting a better following from the local Pittsburgh media. I don't remember if WTAE came to Vegas for the Holyfield fight, but Sam Nover was there for WPXI.

Keep in mind that this was 1994, when the Heavyweight Championship of the World meant something. If Moorer could pull off an upset, he would become the most accomplished international sports figure from Western Pennsylvania since Arnold Palmer.

He also would become the most famous athlete ever to represent Western Pennsylvania.

They've never heard of Arnold Palmer in Russia

They've never heard of Roberto Clemente in Sweden.

They've never heard of Terry Bradshaw in South Africa and they've never heard of Sidney Crosby in Brazil.

In 1994 being the Heavyweight Champ was still a huge deal and it made you a world-famous celebrity.

• • •

Michael Moorer was given very little chance against Evander Holyfield.

But there was that southpaw advantage.

Moorer was then being trained by one of the great characters in boxing, Teddy Atlas. He had a scar that ran from his forehead across his cheek to his chin, a thick New York accent and no patience for Michael Moorer's bullshit.

Moorer had developed a reputation for being tough to handle. Holyfield would find out that Moorer could be even tougher to handle in the ring. Moorer fought a smart fight and tortured Holyfield with right-handed jabs that were confusing to a guy who was used to defending only left-handed jabs.

As the bell rang to end the fight, the boxing writer for a Las Vegas newspaper, who knew that I was from Pittsburgh, jumped out of his seat, ran toward me and shouted, "Moorer won the fight." The writer had been scoring the fight and giving me thumbs-up signs after rounds that he thought were won by Moorer.

Michael Moorer from Monessen, Pa., was the undefeated, undisputed

Heavyweight Champion of the World.

Say what you want about the state of boxing now or the state of boxing in 1994. There is only one real heavyweight champion on the planet. (Don't bore me with the WBCs and WBAs and the IBLs – Moorer was the undisputed heavyweight champ.)

For someone to start out at 11 years old with the goal of becoming what only one human on the face of the Earth can be at any given time, and achieving it, is a stupendous accomplishment. I don't care where you're from or where you say you're from. It's kind of like being an altar boy, aspiring to be the Pope and then becoming the Pope. It's happened to very few people in the history of the planet.

I'm not ashamed to say that I was rooting hard for Moorer that night. And I'm not ashamed to say that I had my own selfish reasons. I had made that prediction to my news director and general manager at KDKA and a win would make me look pretty smart and it would justify the thousands of dollars we had spent.

I was also rooting for Moorer because I had gotten to know him and had seen how hard he had been working and because of one other thing that I'm not ashamed to admit. I thought it was pretty cool to be on the inside with the Heavyweight Champion of the World — one of the most famous people on the planet.

Not long after winning the title, Moorer came to Monessen for a parade in his honor. That made him an official local story, but both he and his handlers were still reluctant to identify too much with Western Pennsylvania.

Moorer's win over Holyfield should have put him in the same class as Joe Montana, Dan Marino, Stan Musial, Johnny Unitas and Arnold Palmer, but it never did.

And he would only be the champ for seven more months.

George Foreman was next.

Foreman had come all the way back from being a 300-pound has-been to a legitimate contender for the heavyweight championship at the age of 45. Three years earlier he had gone the distance and lost in a title fight with Evander Holyfield.

Early in his career, Foreman almost caused my wife Jeani and me to divorce. In 1974 I was living on unemployment in between baseball seasons in Sharon, Pa., when Foreman fought Muhammad Ali in Zaire, Africa. I was a huge Ali fan and there was no way I was going to miss the closed-circuit telecast of "The Rumble in the Jungle."

I took $20 we didn't have and drove from Sharon to Pittsburgh to watch the fight in a Hilton Hotel ballroom. Jeani and I had a huge fight. She, of course, was perfectly justified in saying that we couldn't afford it, but I knew that if I went to see the fight, 20 or 30 years later I would have the memory and the 20 bucks wouldn't matter.

I was right, of course.

So, here I was in Las Vegas on Nov. 5, 1994, exactly 20 years later, covering Foreman's attempt to win back the title and Jeani was there with me.

Foreman was the media darling and the lovable underdog.

Moorer was the standoffish, reluctant champion who was still claiming to be from Detroit. He was also a huge favorite in the fight.

What makes a heavyweight title fight special is the fact that it's a worldwide event. That would hit home at every pre-fight press conference when you would hear questions being asked in many different accents. I would check out the picture-ID credentials hanging around reporters' necks to see how many countries were represented and they were there from all over the world.

For nine rounds Moorer bounced big punches off Foreman's bald head. He was leading on all three judges cards and was on his way to his first successful title defense until …

Boom, BOOM.

A left jab followed by a short right cross and Moorer was down and out. Foreman was Heavyweight Champion and the sports story of the year. Moorer was a trivia answer.

It happened that fast and it was seen all over the world.

Moorer's trainer, Teddy Atlas, had told Moorer to stay away from Foreman. Atlas knew that Foreman still had a big punch.

At the post-fight press conference Moorer said, "They can tell you to stay away from George Foreman, but it's not that easy."

Foreman's boxing shorts were almost as old as the guy he beat to win back his title. They were the same shorts that he wore for the "Rumble in the Jungle" 20 years earlier.

Moorer also said at the press conference that boxing had stopped being fun. "Before this fight I was contemplating retirement," he said. "I've been doing this 14 years. I'll be 27 on the twelfth of this month."

I had arranged with Moorer to meet him after the fight for a one-on-one interview, but I had also assumed that he would win.

I didn't know what his reaction would be when I approached him after the fight as he was getting in the back seat of a car to go to the hospital for a check up.

He saw me in the crowd, put his window down, leaned out and said, "Stag, meet in my room" and gave me the room number.

So, cameraman Michael Challik and I headed for his hotel room. We ended up sitting in the hall outside Moorer's room for a few hours. Then at about 2:30 in the morning the elevator doors open and Moorer, alone and still holding the ice pack to his fat lip, slowly walks down the hall, silently shakes our hands, opens the door and invites us in.

I remember thinking how far away this was from that boxing ring down the street. A few hours earlier, this guy had entered the ring to loud music and a roaring crowd, surrounded by his entourage with millions and millions of people all over the world watching him.

And here he was in the middle of the night, with a swollen face, sitting in his hotel room while the rest of the world was talking about what a great story his loss was.

Great for George Foreman, of course.

Not great at all for Michael Moorer.

It wasn't just losing a title fight that was a new experience for him. He hadn't lost *any* fight in something like 13 years. In a little more than a whisper he said, "I've been doin' this for 15 years. I get so tired of it sometimes. Same routine over and over again. If I was gonna win this fight, then the anticipation of another fight and then the training regimen and all of that. Just so repetitive after a while."

I always had more respect for boxers and wrestlers than I had for other athletes because of what Moorer described. The training is so hard and so tedious and it goes on forever. And then it comes down to you against the other guy in the ring in front of the whole world.

"What will you do tomorrow and for the next week?" I asked Moorer.

"Heal," he said. "Heal up a little. I don't know what I'll do. I'm gonna see my son. Because he cried … 'Daddy fall.' That hurt a little bit. That's what hurt me the most. He don't really know what's goin' on … I guess he does now, seeing his daddy fall. His feelings were hurt."

Being in that room that night with Moorer was one of those moments that made me really appreciate my job.

A few hours earlier, this guy had been the focus of a spectacle that was watched by millions around the world. People in Japan, Germany and the UK would be reading the stories that were written by those guys I saw at the press conferences during the week and I was the only guy on the planet who had the opportunity to talk to him face-to-face about how it felt being on the wrong side of one of the biggest upsets in sports history.

It wasn't long after the Foreman-Moorer fight that the Heavyweight Division became a joke. Foreman was forced to vacate the IBF title because he wouldn't give Axel Schultz, whom he had beaten in a controversial decision, a rematch. Moorer won the IBF title by beating Schulz and that was the beginning of the alphabet lunacy that has made boxing a fringe sport and a joke.

In 1997, Moorer was knocked down five times in a rematch with Holyfield and the fight was stopped after 8 rounds. Moorer retired for three years, came back and beat a couple of tomato cans, was knocked out in 30 seconds by David Tua, continued to hang around and finally fought for the last time in 2008.

For the past few years, Moorer has been working as a trainer.

In my mind, Michael Moorer never did a good enough job of identifying with his hometown and he didn't cooperate with my plan to make him a huge local story, but I won't hold that against him.

I'm just glad I got to go along on his ride.

WHILE WE'RE ON THE SUBJECT
MY JAY LENO MOMENT

Everybody should see Las Vegas at least once.

I made my first trip there for the Michael Moorer-Mike White fight in 1992. I was impressed, but I also knew that I would never come back if I had to pay my own way. I enjoyed being there on an expense account, but when you don't drink and don't gamble, Las Vegas is a lot of lights and a lot of guys with pinky rings and ugly loafers.

I was spoiled, of course, because all my trips there were on KDKA's dime and I got the VIP treatment. The hotels love TV crews because they send back pretty pictures that produce future suckers for their casinos.

On all of my trips, the cameraman, the producer and I were all given free tickets to the shows that were playing during our stay.

Jay Leno was playing Caesar's Palace that week in 1992 and the PR lady gave me, cameraman Michael Challik and producer Bruce Shepman free tickets to Leno's show.

When we presented our tickets at the door, we were escorted down the aisle, past all the guys with the pinky rings and the over-dressed women and directly to the front row.

And I mean front row. I could actually lean on the stage.

Leno was surprisingly funny — much funnier than his average "Tonight Show" monologue. He told a story about going back home to Boston to visit his parents.

Not long after he arrived at his parents house, his dad told him about a cracked toilet seat in one of the bathrooms. Leno described how his dad started searching for a lifetime warranty that he knew he had saved when he bought the seat 25 years earlier.

Leno got a lot of mileage and a lot of laughs out of the story, including a description of his trip to the hardware store with his dad carrying the cracked toilet seat and the old, faded warranty and the crowd loved it.

A few minutes into the act Leno started getting laughs by throwing questions at the people in the audience.

"Where are you from?"

"What do you do for a living?"

You've seen him interact with the audience on "The Tonight Show." The three of us KDKA guys were easy targets in the front row.

Leno looked at Bruce Shepman and asked him what he did for a living. Bruce said, "I'm a TV producer."

Leno threw his hands in the air and yelled out, "Oh, sure you are. Every guy in Vegas is a TV producer. How many women have bought that line so far?"

He got a big laugh.

I was hoping that Leno would ask me what I did for a living because

I had an answer ready for him.

Leno looked me in the eye and said, "OK. Let's hear it. Your buddy's a big-time TV producer. What do you do for a living, casting director?"

"No," I said, "I'm a salesman for the Eljer toilet seat company."

It got one of the bigger laughs of the night and Leno said, "OK, smart guy. I'll do the jokes around here if you don't mind."

It was one of my better adlibs.

CHAPTER 24

QUOTES FROM THE UNFAMOUS

When my mother (Kay) was about 85 years old, she had to spend a few days in the hospital for minor surgery. My dad (Bill), who was about 83 at the time, was pushing her in a wheelchair to the pick-up area in front of the hospital. As he headed out the door toward the curb, my dad noticed that there was a crowd of 20 or 30 people there and they were all watching him. He stopped, turned to them, smiled and said, "It's a boy!"

CHAPTER 25

TALKIN' TALK RADIO

I've never had a boss tell me he loved me more often than Jim Meltzer. There were times when I would pass him in the hall and he would go on and on about how much he loved my new radio talk show and I was afraid that he was going to kiss me.

The fact that I only lasted six months in that job should tell you something about the joys of working in radio.

It was the spring of 2007 and Meltzer was the general manager of 93.7 FM, one of CBS' four radio stations in Pittsburgh. In April the station launched "The Zone," a format that was called "The Man Station" and targeted at Pittsburgh men between 25-49. 93.7 The Zone began with big ideas and high hopes but was pulled off the air in October.

I was part of a good lineup. Opie & Anthony's nationally syndicated show ran from 6-9 a.m., followed by me from nine until 10. Then it was Dennis Miller's syndicated talk show from 10 until 1 p.m., followed by Pittsburghers John McIntire and Scott Paulsen.

I loved my hour-long show and busted my ass to make it good and different. I'm pretty sure I was the first — and last — guy in the history of talk radio to combine sports, politics and entertainment in a one-hour talk show.

That's why the boss liked it so much.

I did it like a TV show, broken into three 20-minute segments. I could be talking about the Penguins in the playoffs in the first 20 minutes, national or local politics in the second 20 and "American Idol" in the last

20. It left me very little room to take calls, and that's another reason why I think Meltzer, who had been in radio a hundred years, loved it.

My show was working. We didn't have the numbers to prove it yet, but when you have a recognizable face from TV and you're working in radio, you can judge how you're doing based on the feedback and I was getting lots of it and it was positive.

I was still doing TV in 2007 and that meant some long days, especially when you consider that I was getting up every day at 5 a.m. to prepare for my hour show. A lot of my time at KDKA was spent trying to line up radio guests for the next day.

I started at 93.7 The Zone in April as a part-timer and the plan was for me to go full-time on the radio when my TV contract at KDKA expired in October 2007.

Early on October 1, just before I was scheduled to go on 93.7 The Zone full time, I got an email from Keith Clark, the guy who oversaw programming at all of the CBS Radio stations in Pittsburgh. He wanted me to stop in his office before I went on the air that day. I figured he was going to tell me that my show was going to be expanding, which I had been told to expect a couple of months earlier.

I did my usual prep work and showed up at the CBS Radio office in Green Tree at about 8:15 the morning of October 1.

Keith looked pained.

The Zone was his baby. He had big plans for it and was sure that it was going to succeed in Pittsburgh. Unfortunately, the CBS suits in New York didn't agree.

They had made the decision to pull the plug on all of the network's Man Stations and, even though we were showing signs of progress and hadn't been given anything close to a fair chance to succeed, The Zone was history.

Starting that day 93.7 FM would be playing automated Christmas music until a rock format was installed. I had done my preparation that morning for nothing. I had no talk show to do. The plug had already been pulled. Lots of good people lost their jobs.

I was an unemployed full-time radio employee before I got a chance to be a full time radio employee. My contract with 93.7 The Zone would pay me for a year to do nothing, which was a new experience for me.

WORKING FOR THE BIG "K"

Trust me. I never had aspirations to do a general talk show on KDKA Radio. But management decided that since they were paying me and Scott Paulsen to do nothing after the plug was pulled on 93.7 the Zone, they would ask us if we would like to do a show together from 7-10 p.m.

Keep in mind, both of us could be paid to do nothing for a year.

We both asked for a little more money and agreed to go on the air in January of 2008. Scott had only recently escaped from the nightshift at WDVE and had no interest in working in that time slot long term and he let KDKA management know that he would only do the show until April unless he was moved to a daytime shift.

Fred Honsberger was very sick and housebound at the time and we thought we might be offered a show in his afternoon-drive spot, but Fred hung on for another year and Paulsen was gone April 1.

That's when I, your friendly sportscaster, was given an opportunity to do a general talk show on the 50,000-Watt Blow Torch.

Seven months before a presidential election.

Talk about jumping into the fire.

I had no doubts about being able to pull it off because I knew I was more than conversant enough in politics and had done some political talk on The Zone.

Working for KDKA was different from working for The Zone. For one thing, instead of a nice new office and shiny new studio in an office park in Green Tree, at KDKA I got a depressing, old office in Gateway Center and a radio studio that should have been condemned by the Allegheny County Health Department.

KDKA finally moved to Green Tree to join the other CBS Stations in 2010, but I ended up spending nine and a half months in a studio that looked almost the same as it did when Rege Cordic was doing his morning show in 1956.

It wasn't just old. It was dirty. I know that I was sitting in close proximity to dandruff that had fallen from Cordic's head when Ike was president.

Every night, as I sat there for three hours doing my show, I would look around and think about how shocked the people listening would be if they knew what a rat hole I was working in.

KDKA's call letters are iconic and I would think that listeners pictured me sitting in a posh studio, in a big leather chair surrounded by lots of stainless steel, chrome and glass.

I was surrounded by dirt and sitting in a chair that I couldn't slide from one side of the controls to the other because of a hole in the floor. From what I could tell, the hole had been there since KDKA's first broadcast in 1920.

I also found out that most of the callers had been listening since those Harding-Cox election returns. With few exceptions, most nights I took calls from the same 12 people, most of whom were at least 70 years old. Not that there's anything wrong with old listeners, but I was 60 and I felt like a kid talking to most of these people.

When Myron Cope was at the peak of his popularity, he established a rule that limited listeners to one call per week. He was ahead of his time. If I had limited listeners to one call per week, I think I would have been totally caller-less by Tuesday.

Even though I was busting my ass preparing for each show with almost no help, I enjoyed it and the people I worked for and with couldn't have been nicer or more professional. Fred Honsberger and Marty Griffin had their own producers. Even though their producers were more than happy to help me when they could, I was pretty much on my own. I picked my topics and booked virtually all of my guests.

HOW TO SPOT A LAZY TALK-SHOW HOST

I had been working mostly in TV for 29 years before making the move back to radio. But I had enough experience doing talk shows, including working as a fill-in for both Myron Cope and Stan Savran at WTAE radio, to have an idea how to prepare for one. I also learned how to spot a lazy radio talk-show host.

If you hear a guy on the air say "Let me know what you think" more than three times an hour, that's a pretty good sign that he's done nothing to prepare for his show.

With 93.7 The Fan in Pittsburgh, which went on the air in February of 2010, we have an example of a lousy talk show *station*. It's obvious from listening to it that the bosses think that phone calls bring ratings.

I disagree.

The thing that talk-show callers do more than anything else is bring the talk-show to a screeching halt.

There are times when a major controversy erupts or a coach is fired when the host should open the phone lines and let it rip. But when you hear your favorite radio voice say "What do you think?" or "I'd like your take on this," that usually means that he thought of the topic for the hour about 11 seconds before he opened his mic.

What are the chances that you're going to hear scintillating, provocative stories when the host says, "So, what's your favorite chip to eat when you watch a game?" I didn't hear that but I was told that that question was actually asked by a host a few months after The Fan went on the air.

Rush Limbaugh is the most successful radio talk-show host ever and I'd be willing to bet that he hasn't said "Let me hear how you feel about it" to his audience two times in more than 20 years.

A good host, who's earning his salary, goes into the studio with guests booked to cover every minute of his shift or with material that he prepared for a few hours before the show that will allow him to fill the time with interesting topics and opinions without begging callers to bail him out and do his show for him.

Pittsburgh talk radio has evolved a lot since the days of Ed and Wendy King on KDKA in the mid '50s. Ed and Wendy would take phone calls every night but you wouldn't hear them. Wendy would say, "Ed, a caller has a backed-up toilet and is looking for a quick way to get it working again." Ed would then either give his advice or ask listeners to call in. The listener, of course, had to take Ed and Wendy's word for it that there was actually a caller. For all we know they made half of them up.

In the mid-'60s, WJAS went to a news/talk format that included callers that you could actually hear. Tom Bender had the first real sports talk show in Pittsburgh on WTAE in 1970 and he was replaced after one year by Myron Cope.

There's a lot more sports talk on the air now but that doesn't mean it's better. Myron and Stan Savran were as good as it gets and they each did one hour a night. It's a lot to ask anybody — even a two-man team — to do four good hours of talk radio without having to be reduced to asking people for a chip preference.

• • •

My experience doing a talk show at KDKA should give you an idea of how ridiculous radio can be.

When I agreed to take extra money on top of what I was owed on my one-year contract with The Zone — to do the 7-10 p.m. shift on KDKA — I was told by CBS Pittsburgh VP of Programming Keith Clark (not his real name; more on that in a minute) that at the end of one year the money would have to be a lot less. I said OK, knowing that there was little chance that I would accept a pay cut.

In November of 2008 I went to the news director at KDKA Radio, Marshal Adams (not his real name; more on that in a minute). I told him that when my talk-show contract was up in a little over three months, I had no interest whatsoever in continuing to do the same job for less money. I was working too hard to accept a dime less than what I was getting. "Marshall Adams" said that he understood and that my show wasn't even on his radar and thanked me for the heads up.

Two weeks later I got a call to come in early on a Monday afternoon. Uh, oh.

I was told my show, which I thought was doing well, would no longer be on the air. I would get a nice four-month paid vacation. I thanked Marshall (not his real name) and KDKA's General Manager Michael Young (as far as I know, his real name), and that was that.

Mike Pintek, who had been fired two years earlier by KDKA, was hired to take my place. I thought it was kind of strange that KDKA would bring back a guy they had just fired, but a few weeks later I got the explanation from Keith Clark (not his real name.)

The CBS affiliate in Baltimore had just hired Pintek to do a general-topic talk show. Two weeks after he was hired, CBS decided to turn the station that hired Pintek into an all-sports station similar to what would eventually happen to 93.7 in Pittsburgh when it became 93.7 The Fan.

So CBS Radio was faced with a guy who told them he wasn't going to work beyond his current contract for less money (me) and a guy who had to be paid for almost an entire year for doing nothing (Pintek).

Whatever it was that the people at KDKA didn't like about Mike Pintek when they fired him suddenly didn't bother them at all. Pintek signed on to do four hours of talk instead of three for, I would assume, less money than they were paying me.

Good for Mike Pintek, whom I've always liked, and good for me

KDKA's ratings are in the toilet in 2011, unless you're talking about the 75-to-laid-out-at-Beinhauer's Funeral Home demographic, and it may decide to come into the 21st century some time soon.

I figure that at least four of the 12 regular callers to my show in 2008 are now dead. I have my doubts that they've been replaced.

NEW DEMOGRAPHICS

It may be time for radio stations to change their thinking a little bit on their demographic targets — at least in the Pittsburgh market. Remember that I said The Zone was targeted to men aged 25 to 49? Does that make sense in 2011? Do 28-year-olds really have the same interests as 48-year-olds?

How many 48-year-olds — men and women — have tattoos compared to 28-year-olds?

Those old demographic targets were used mostly for music stations. That's why the ages 18 to 35 and 25 to 54 made sense. But in the Age of the iPod, people are becoming less and less dependent on radio for their music. Talk and information are the future of radio and it's time that the programmers, especially in the Pittsburgh market, where there is a huge segment of the population over 45, understood that it's not 1965 anymore.

It no longer makes sense to consider anyone over 54 to be dead when it comes to appealing to advertisers. Once a Chevy man always a Chevy man may have been true of my dad's generation, but it sure as hell isn't true of mine.

Sixty-year olds are willing to try new products and they have the money to spend on them. They listen to talk radio and they're not like the 60-year-olds of their fathers' generation.

They don't wear the same shirts and ties that they wore when they were in college and they drive SUVs, sports cars and convertibles. Not four-door sedans.

They work out and walk around in t-shirts and flip-flops.

I have more than one 60-plus friend who could beat the shit out of 80 percent of the 20-somethings in the city. (Eighty percent of the 60-year-olds in the city could have beaten the shit out of me when I was 20-something.)

Nobody in radio is talking to this older demographic. It's as though the programmers think that we're all out here sitting on a front porch playing gin rummy with the old geezer from across the street. That may have been happening in 1965, but it's not happening now.

What's funny is that 40 years ago I wrote a letter to the general manager of WDVE Radio in Pittsburgh and tried to convince him that not everybody who was listening to Album Rock radio was high on acid and living in a commune. I tried to sell him on the idea that sports fans listened to rock music, too.

Five years later, in 1977, I became WDVE's first sports guy.

RADIO ALIASES

Imagine you're working for, say, PNC Bank, and about six months into the job you find out that the guy who hired you, Kirby King, isn't really named Kirby King. Would you think it was kind of strange that a guy would use a name other than his own at work?

Would you wonder if his wife called him by his real name or his bank name?

Keith Clark, the vice president of programming at KDKA Radio couldn't have been nicer to me. He hired me for The Zone and he was one of my biggest boosters, but I have to say that it was a little strange when I found out that Keith Clark wasn't his real name.

I understand disc jockeys using stage names. It happens all the time in radio. But I found it a little weird that a VP of programming would.

So imagine how disturbing it was to also find out that the news director at KDKA Radio was using an alias. Marshal Adams was not really Marshall Adams. During my time there he got married and I wondered if he actually said "I, Marshall Adams take thee ..." or if he used his real name.

I was told both of their real names, but I don't remember them.

I wouldn't tell you, anyway.

Wouldn't want to blow their cover. Lives could be at stake.

WHILE WE'RE ON THE SUBJECT

Early in 2010, I had some conversations with the general manager at 93.7 The Fan, Terry Foxx, about doing some work there. It never materialized and I found out a few weeks after my conversations with him that Foxx was not Terry's last name.

Those two "Xs" should have been a dead giveaway.

IRRELEVANT RADIO

Radio stations are about to become irrelevant. Not in the next two weeks, but quite possibly in your lifetime. Since January of 2011, I have been hosting a sports talk show on something called TribLive Radio. It's on the Pittsburgh Tribune-Review's website and it's also the future of radio.

For the last 80 years, KDKA Radio has had a huge advantage in the Pittsburgh market because the FCC allowed it to broadcast at 50,000 watts. That gave KDKA the power to be heard in 39 states, but more important it gave KDKA a huge advantage locally because it could continue to pump out 50,000 watts at night when the other stations were required by the FCC to power down to as low as 1,000 watts.

About 10 years ago, I hosted a sports talk show on 970 AM that was sponsored by the Trib. The signal barely made it out of Green Tree, where the station was located. There are people in Egypt who have listened to my current show on TribLive Radio. Towers and signal strength still matter right now, but because of the Internet pretty soon it's going to be all about who has the best content.

For about a hundred bucks, you can buy a radio that will allow you to listen to every Internet radio station on the planet and carmakers are already including Internet access in their electronic packages.

It will be a while before every car is equipped with an Internet radio, but when that happens, the party is over for the KDKAs of the world. Satellite radio (one of the greatest inventions in human history) is now being offered in most new cars and will continue to grow. That's commercial-free and static-free radio that can be heard anywhere on the planet.

Instead of the millions of dollars spent on elaborate studios and tall transmitters and the humans required to maintain them, all you need to start your own radio station is a laptop computer, a telephone and less than $2,000 in equipment.

No stupid FCC rules.

No getting blown out by another station's stronger signal.

Just you and your microphone sitting in your basement or your bedroom and you have a worldwide audience.

Whether you use your real name is totally up to you.

CHAPTER 26

SHORT STOP

FLYING WITH THE KING

Early in my TV career, I established myself as an idea man. I was pretty good at coming up with good ideas for stories. Sometimes it wasn't as much about originality as it was about thinking big.

For example, in 1995, KDKA News Director Sue McInerney came to the sports department and asked us to give her a list of former Steelers to contact about working for us as an analyst during Super Bowl week in Phoenix.

The usual names were thrown around — Jack Ham, Rocky Bleier, Lynn Swann, Franco Harris, Dwight White, L.C. Greenwood, Mike Wagner — and any one of them would have helped the ratings and done an excellent job.

I remember thinking that the other two stations would be going after the same guys and it took me about 15 seconds before I blurted out, "How about Chuck Noll?"

Noll was not known for his interest in getting TV face time. I would guess that in his 23 years as head coach of the Steelers he didn't make three appearances on a talk show. I called him and he said he was interested.

The word was that he got $10,000 to be live on our 5 and 11 p.m. newscasts that week and he was excellent.

In January of 1980, 13 months into my job at WTAE, I came up with one of my better ideas. To me it was a no-brainer. The Steelers had just won the Super Bowl and the Pirates had won the World Series in October. We were an ABC affiliate and ABC had a show called "Superstars." It was a decathlon-like competition between superstar athletes from different sports. (Joe Frazier swimming was one of my favorite moments.)

In February, ABC would have the Super Bowl and World Series winners compete against each other. I went to the WTAE news director and I said, "This will be the only time in history that the Pirates and Steelers compete against each other on national TV. We have to be there."

Again, that may seem like a no-brainer to you, but when I suggested it, I was stunned by how much credit I got for coming up with a brilliant idea.

I was also a little stunned when they decided to send Bill Hillgrove to Hawaii to cover it. Myron Cope also went along to write a story for Sports Illustrated, which meant that I stayed home and covered for Bill on TV and hosted Myron's radio show.

My idea got them a week in Hawaii and me an extra-heavy work week in Wilkinsburg.

In 1983, the U.S. Open was at Oakmont Country Club and it was an ABC event. The sales department saw the opportunity to make lots of money with a U.S. Open show and the sports department was told to come up with some ideas to fill it.

Eleven years earlier I had covered the Firestone Classic in Akron for WKSU Radio — the Kent State FM station. It was my first sports event on a press pass and I had been really impressed when Arnold Palmer did a low fly-by in his jet and tipped his wings to the huge gallery waiting on the 18th hole as the leader, Jerry Heard, was making his way up the fairway.

I suggested going for a ride in Arnie's jet.

Palmer's PR guy Doc Giffin thought it was an excellent idea and it was arranged for me to fly with him to the Memorial Tournament in Columbus the week before the U.S. Open came to Oakmont. We were told to be at Latrobe Airport at 6 a.m.

We were standing by Arnie's jet when he pulled up in his Cadillac, took his clubs out of the trunk and put them in the jet, looked at us and gestured for us to get on board.

A co-pilot was required on his plane and I learned that Arnie left most of the flying to his pilot, but he agreed to take the yoke for the purposes of our story. We got some good shots of Arnie in the cockpit and I think he did a few cowboy moves to impress and/or scare us, but he really didn't say much.

After about 30 minutes in the air we landed in Columbus. Arnie took his clubs out of the jet and threw them in the trunk of another Cadillac and drove off. It was up to us to get to the golf course in time to see him tee off.

We also got to see him teed off.

He three-putted all over the place, shot 81 and missed the cut. He wasn't real talkative at the airport when we were boarding the jet for the return trip. In fact, he didn't say a word.

Arnie was 53 and long past the point where he was expected to be a factor at a major PGA Tour stop, but it was pretty obvious that he expected a lot more out of himself than the rest of the golf world did.

I wish I could tell you that Arnie was a lot of fun to fly with, but he wasn't. I have to admit I was expecting him to be a little more cooperative, but he didn't seem all that interested.

At the time I remember being a little disappointed. Now I realize that it was because he was still Arnold Palmer, this was a business trip and when it came to golf, even at his advanced age, he was all business.

Missing the cut *really* pissed him off.

WHILE WE'RE ON THE SUBJECT

I was so impressed by my trip in Arnie's jet that I decided to take flying lessons. I really liked the freedom and power that comes with flying above the traffic.

I had also lived with a minor fear of flying. It never prevented me from getting on a plane, but I was annoyed by the fact that little noises or bumpy rides worried me too much.

Learning to fly a plane is the best way to cure a fear of being a passenger in one.

I took my lessons from Neal Spence, who had been doing radio traffic reports for many years. Neal suggested that I go with him during one of his morning flights to see if I liked it. I had never been in a small plane and he let me take the yoke once we got in the air.

He told me that he was putting it in neutral (there may be another aeronautical word for it, but you get the drift) and he said, "The only way this plane is going to fall out of the sky is if you make it fall."

I loved it and started showing up two or three times a week for my lesson. After a while, during his radio traffic reports, Neal would turn it over to me and I would take the plane wherever I wanted. We would be flying over I-79 North and Neal would give his description of what was happening on the Parkway East. I noticed that he got a lot of his information from people on the ground and didn't really need to be actually flying over the area he was reporting on.

My official lesson would start after he had done his traffic reports. One day, after a few weeks of doing lots of touch-and-goes — bringing the plane in for a landing and then, before coming to a complete stop, taking off again — Neal got out of the plane and said, "You're on your own."

Solo time.

What a feeling.

I actually remember letting out a loud yell when I felt the wheels leave the ground and realized that I was actually flying an airplane by myself.

I did a few touch-and-goes by myself, got my congratulations from the guys in the control tower and Neal, and I had a huge smile on my face all the way home.

I never soloed again.

The more I learned about flying, the more I realized it wasn't for me. I'm the kind of guy who can park a car in the lot in the morning and forget to shut it off. It's a little different when you're flying a plane. Being absent-minded or inattentive means death.

I'll never forget that one and only solo flight and I no longer worry about those little noises and little bumps.

WHILE WE'RE STILL ON THE SUBJECT

Every time I hear or read about a plane crash, I remember something that Neal Spence told me. "Notice how often you hear or read the words rain, snow, fog, storm or wind in any story about a plane crash —especially a small plane," he said.

You'll see or hear some word related to bad weather almost 100 percent of the time when it's a story about a small plane crash. As Neal said, you have to make the plane fall out of the sky and one good way to do that is to fly in conditions that you shouldn't be flying in.

To this day, when I'm reading a story about a plane crash I take note of how far I have to go into the story before I see one of Neal's words. I rarely have to go more than three sentences.

CHAPTER 27

SHORT STOP

WEDDING BALLS

You probably never noticed that Dan Marino went most of his NFL career without showing up on KDKA-TV. I guess it's ironic that he's now on KDKA-TV every Sunday as a panelist on CBS' "NFL Today."

Marino's problem was a classic case of a TV news department sticking its nose in the sports department and screwing up not only a story but a long-term relationship.

It was late in 1984 and word got out that Dan Marino was getting married. Marino was a huge deal at the time. He was coming off the most successful rookie season in NFL history in 1983, was named MVP in 1984 when he set several NFL passing records and he was on his way to the Super Bowl in Palo Alto, California. And, of course, he was a Pittsburgh kid.

I was working at WTAE then and I remember the news director popping his head into the sports office and asking, "What are you guys going to do with the Marino wedding?"

In unison, Stan Savran, producer Tim Kiely and I said, "Nothing."

We made it clear that they should send a female news reporter — Debra Fox or Sally Wiggin — because we wanted no part of it.

One big reason for our unanimous rejection of the idea was that we just had no interest in covering a wedding.

We didn't care if Dan Marino ever got married. But we also knew that Marino was not the most media-friendly athlete around and that he guarded his privacy ferociously and would not want TV cameras in his face on his wedding day.

And we also figured he was going to be around the NFL for the next 15 years or so and it wouldn't be smart to sour a relationship over some stupid wedding shots. Our news department at WTAE was smart enough to understand and decided to keep the sports department out of Marino's wedding.

I did make the mistake of letting some people in the newsroom know that Marino was marrying my second cousin. When I went to Palo Alto for the Super Bowl, I was under orders to do what I could to get an interview with his soon-to-be wife, Claire.

She is the daughter of my first cousin, who happens to be about 20 years older than I am and whom I hadn't seen or spoken to since I was about eight years old. I didn't remember ever speaking to Claire and I had no interest whatsoever in interviewing her.

I put the interview request in with someone in the Dolphins' media relations department and in the process made it clear that I would be perfectly happy if he said no.

Keep in mind that this is in the middle of the Super Bowl media circus.

A day or two later I got a call from Marino. He said that neither Claire nor he would be interested in being interviewed. I made it clear to him that I was hoping he would say no and that I had only put in the request to cover my ass. He was very understanding and I thanked him and wished him good luck against the 49ers.

KDKA was not so smart.

Marino practically begged the media to leave him alone on his wedding day and both WTAE and WPXI kept their coverage to a minimum. But somebody at KDKA decided to aggressively try to get "close to the action."

A KDKA-TV news car and a reporter were posted outside Marino's parents' house in Oakland. (It might have been sports reporter Alan Cutler, who, at the time, was the last person in Pittsburgh you'd want parked outside your home.) Marino was videotaped leaving in his tux and getting into a limo. I would love to have a still shot of the look on Marino's face when he saw the camera.

If that wasn't intrusive enough, KDKA bribed Marino's wedding videographer and he made copies of the video he shot of the actual wedding ceremony, including some really nice close-ups of the couple exchanging their vows — with audio — that were aired on Channel 2 that night.

KDKA won the prize that day, but Marino said he would never speak to KDKA again. And, as far as I know, he didn't for the rest of his career. I do know that I went to work at KDKA a year later and it was understood for years and years that if Marino came to Pittsburgh for a function or to play the Steelers, it was a waste of time to ask him to do an interview.

I never blamed Marino one bit.

It was a stupid move by the KDKA news department. It would have been different if Marino were in town to go on trial for committing a crime. Then he would be fair game. But he asked for some privacy on his wedding day and KDKA couldn't back off.

Sometimes you have to measure the value of pissing somebody off to get a scoop against putting yourself at a disadvantage with your competition for 10 or 15 years.

Marino never had much patience with the media. If I were to pick a word to describe his mood almost every time I saw him, I'd say "surly." He thought a lot of the questions were stupid and never really seemed to understand why people were so interested in his innermost thoughts.

He just wanted to throw the football.

I think where he grew up had a lot to do with that. Marino is the quintessential Pittsburgh Guy. Not interested in being phony and not all that interested in letting someone else decide how he should feel about himself.

Of course, now that he works for CBS, he finds himself sitting down with NFL quarterbacks and asking the same stupid questions that he had no patience for. He's not the first media-unfriendly star to find himself in that position. Those guys learn early on that some of those questions that seem stupid can elicit pretty good answers.

Another thing that athletes never seem to get is that when they're sitting at home watching "SportsCenter" and hearing sound-bites that they find interesting, they're actually hearing answers to questions that they would have considered stupid.

In 2000 I went to Miami for Marino's retirement announcement and KDKA was the only local Pittsburgh television station there. Marino noticed me in the huge crowd of people and cameras and thanked me for coming. I had asked his dad, Dan Sr., earlier if he could set up a one-on-one interview and he said he didn't think it would be a problem.

When the press conference ended, Dan Sr. came up to me in the parking lot and said that Junior wasn't interested in doing the interview. I thought it was strange since he had acknowledged my presence at the press conference and thanked me for coming. (I never did think that my mother's brother being his wife's grandfather would be a factor in his decision.)

Was that snub one last payback for what KDKA did on his wedding day 16 years earlier?

Maybe.

If it was, I don't blame Marino one bit.

WHILE WE'RE ON THE SUBJECT

By the way, that relative that Claire Marino and I share is a guy who left more of a mark on Pittsburgh than Dan. His name was Larry Hatch and he opened a little restaurant on Saw Mill Run Boulevard back in 1949 that led to a few other restaurants sprinkled all over Western Pennsylvania.

They're still around today and doing OK.

Maybe you've heard of them or have even eaten in one.

They're called Eat'n Park.

CHAPTER 28

BEHIND THE SCORES (LITERALLY)

If you were alive on Friday, October 13, 1960, you know exactly where you were when Bill Mazeroski led off the bottom of the ninth inning with a home run that won the World Series for the Pirates.

If you weren't alive and you grew up in Western Pennsylvania, you've seen the video a thousand times.

If you weren't alive and you grew up in the United States of America, you've probably seen the video more times than you can count.

Dick Jeffers will never forget where he was that day because, other than Yankees pitcher Ralph Terry, catcher Johnny Blanchard and Maz himself, he came closer to the most famous home run ever hit than any other person at Forbes Field that day.

Stay tuned and you'll find out how.

That's what we used to call a tease in television.

Dick Jeffers' father, John, who everybody called "Jeff," was the scoreboard crew chief at Forbes Field in the '50s and early '60s.

He was in charge of making sure that the Pirates' score and the scores of all the other games in Major League Baseball were posted half-inning-by-half-inning on the big, beautiful, green scoreboard in leftfield.

Who knew that the great Forbes Field scoreboard
housed its own cast of characters?

The scores were displayed by using numbered metal plates that were placed in little windows that corresponded with the inning of each game. I'm guessing you either remember the scoreboard at Forbes Field or have seen pictures of it.

There are very few people still walking the Earth who can say that they were ever inside that scoreboard. Dick Jeffers, better known as "Shakes," is one of them. From the mid-'50s to the early '60s, he went to every Pirates game with his dad and he worked for free. Now 66, "Shakes" was the youngest person working in the scoreboard, which means most if not all of the others who were ever inside it are dead.

According to "Shakes," the scoreboard at Forbes Field was about three stories high and was the biggest of its kind in the Major Leagues. He estimates that its interior was about 15-feet wide and 60-feet long, with six or seven steps up to the first floor and six or seven more steps up to the second floor.

The inside back wall was black and it was covered with players' autographs written with white chalk. On part of that wall, during the years when the Pirates' bullpen was on the leftfield line, former Pirates pitcher Bob Veale would draw large caricatures, including a huge one of Bob Prince that was accompanied by the words "Ocean Mouth."

Inside the scoreboard was a four-man crew that included someone manning the Western Union ticker that delivered the scores of every game being played. The guy watching the ticker (usually "Shakes'" dad) would call the scores down to the guys who were in charge of putting the numbered plates in the various windows.

A guy named Sammy was always in charge of watching the Pirates game and his arms and head could always be seen hanging out of the opening for the bottom of the ninth inning. Visiting teams were always accusing Sammy of stealing their catcher's signs. They thought that his arms moving around were some kind of code for the Pirates' hitters.

"Shakes" says that was never true, although "Shakes" once was thrown out of a game because of a team's complaints. "They had to throw somebody out, so they tossed me instead of the paid help."

Visiting teams became even more suspicious after "Shakes'" dad brought in some German high-powered, World War II binoculars for the crew to play with. How could you blame a visiting manager for suspecting that his signs were being stolen?

"The binoculars were for the players to check out broads in the bleachers," "Shakes" said.

"Shakes" and his dad would enter the ballpark through the concession area on the right-field side and walk through the filthy, disgusting bowels of Forbes Field, dodging rats on their way. "Shakes" says that in those days it was known as "Filthy Forbes" around the National League. The players had to take the same dirty route to get from the clubhouse to their dugouts.

On their way through the concession area, "Shakes" and his dad would pick up a garbage bag of fresh popcorn, 12 or 18 hotdogs and buns, giant pickle jars full of Coke and a couple of large blocks of ice.

That's how they made their money on the side.

The scoreboard crew had its own concession stand inside the scoreboard.

The visitors bullpen was on the left-field line a few feet from the scoreboard entrance and "Shakes'" dad saw to it that the players never went hungry or thirsty.

"They knew that we had food. Mostly on weekends. Especially on Sunday doubleheaders. We doubled up. We knew we would have a lot of house guests."

A player would yell into the door, "Does Jeff have beer today?"

He usually did.

By the entrance to the scoreboard was an empty Coke cup with the word "refreshments" written on it for tips and, according to "Shakes," "If you didn't leave with 50 bucks it was a bad day." (That's $370 dollars in 2010.)

I saw a lot of games at Forbes Field and I can tell you I never looked at that big beautiful scoreboard and imagined visiting players in there drinking beer, smoking cigarettes, grilling hot dogs and looking for beaver shots in the bleachers.

•   •   •

It was known around the National League that the Forbes Field scoreboard was the place to go for in-game refreshments.

"Shakes" talks about the time that Sandy Koufax of the Dodgers was pitching the second game of a doubleheader and the scoreboard filled up with every pitcher in the Dodgers' bullpen.

Koufax had built up a huge lead and everybody in the ballpark knew that he wasn't going to be coming out of the game, so all the guys in the bullpen decided to have a cookout. The bullpen was empty in the sixth inning.

The visitors dugout was on the third-base side in those days and the manager couldn't see his bullpen unless he came up to at least the top of the dugout steps.

When the Pirates started chipping away at Koufax, Dodgers manager Walter Alston picks up the bullpen phone.

No answer.

Alston climbs to the dugout steps and can't see any of his relief pitchers and pretty soon he's standing on third base yelling in the direction of the scoreboard.

"Shakes" was watching through one of the scoreboard windows and yelled down to the Dodgers players below, "Hey, you guys. I think there's a guy out there who's looking for you."

One of the players looked through a window, saw Alston and told his teammates the manager was looking for them.

"It was like a Chinese fire drill, "Shakes" says. "Eight or nine pitchers scrambling out the door and running toward the bullpen."

"Shakes" says that the following day the Pittsburgh Post-Gazette ran a picture of all the pitchers running out of the scoreboard. He also says that the Pirates knocked Koufax out and went on to win the game.

The guys on the scoreboard crew were happy to take care of the visiting team's refreshments and they were well compensated for it, but they also did their best to add to the Pirates' home-field advantage.

For example, there was a space of 10 or 15 feet between the entrance to the scoreboard and the left-field foul line. If a ball made it into that corner, 365 feet from home plate, it would bounce around like a Ping-Pong ball and would often get away from the leftfielder and end up as a triple.

The scoreboard entrance was there and, because there was no door, balls would often carom off the wall and go into the scoreboard for what was supposed to be a ground-rule double.

Not every ball that went inside the scoreboard stayed there, according to "Shakes." "Depends who hits it. If it was a Pirates hitter, and we see it's coming into the scoreboard, we would catch it and throw it back out and see if he could get a triple."

I'm sure, with all the games that I saw at Forbes Field, that I saw at least one triple into that corner that should have been a ground-rule double if not for "Shakes" and the boys.

"One time the visiting leftfielder knew that we had messed with the ball and he calls the dugout from the bullpen phone. The manager protests and the call goes up to the press box. (P.A. announcer) Art McKenna calls the scoreboard and says to my dad, 'Are your kids fucking with the ball?' My dad asks me if I touched the ball. I denied it, but two or three innings later, three of us were thrown out."

"We had to make a long walk down the leftfield line. Guys in the bullpen giving us shit, too."

"Shakes" also did his best to make Bob Skinner of the Pirates a better leftfielder.

"From up there on the second floor of the scoreboard — 20 or 30 feet in the air — I had a pretty good sense of where a ball was going. If I thought that the ball was going to hit the scoreboard, I would yell, 'Off.' Skinner would know that he could turn and play the ball off the scoreboard."

He didn't do that for the visiting leftfielders.

"Fuck no."

Except for Stan Musial.

"He was 'Stan the Man' — a local guy from Donora and an all-time great. Kind of like having Arnold Palmer playing left field. One afternoon game, Musial knocked on one of the windows and asked me to hold his sunglasses. I was shaking in my shoes."

Eventually, "Shakes" noticed that the ushers, led by the legendary "Hooks," who got his name because of a ridiculously large nose and who I bribed many times myself for a good seat on the third-base side at Three Rivers Stadium, decided to set up some folding chairs on a walkway in the leftfield bleachers.

"It was a bunch of Irish and Italian guys from Bloomfield. The chairs were for friends and family. The ushers would let their friends and family in for free and give them prime seating.

"After a while, I found out that most of them were bookies."

For some reason, "Shakes" says, the bookies loved to bet Yankees games. They also paid close attention to the scoreboard. Next to each team's name was the number of the starting pitcher and fans could refer to their scorecards to find out who the pitcher was. That number could be changed by the guys in the scoreboard when the Western Union ticker indicated the team had made a pitching change.

Scoreboard watchers, especially the ones with a financial stake in the games, would perk up when they saw a pitching change because it often meant that a big number was going to go up in the next inning's window.

"Shakes," being a normal teenager, found a way to mess with the bookies and the rest of the crowd by manipulating the score of a Yankees game after posting a new pitcher's number.

"They're waiting to see what the damage was going to be. I would pull out the blank plate and hear the crowd start to buzz. Then I would put a big number in there — a 5 or a 6. The crowd would roar and I would pull it out and put the zero in. I was just pissing around with the bookies.

"One time, Art McKenna called my dad on the scoreboard phone and said, "Your kid is fucking with the Yankees game."

(I do a really good impersonation of Art McKenna, which includes a really good impersonation of the Forbes Field echo. Art was a frail, sweet, little man who was confined to a wheelchair. He had a ridiculously pleasant voice and I can't tell you how funny it is for me when I try to imagine his beautiful, calming voice —which I heard so many times echoing in the Oakland night — being on the other end of a telephone line saying "Your kid's fucking with the Yankees game." If you remember Art's voice, I'm sure it's hard for you to imagine, too.)

After McKenna's call, "Shakes'" dad called him upstairs to the second floor.

"He asked me what I was doing. He didn't think it was all that funny. The visiting players, who were in there at the time, loved it."

I'm sure, with all the games I saw at Forbes Field, I was one of the people who contributed to the buzz or the roar when a big number flashed on the scoreboard and had no idea that it was just "Shakes" "Pissing around with the bookies."

GAME 7

It was standing-room-only inside the scoreboard on October 13, 1960. Game 7 of the World Series.

"Shakes" says there were at least 20 people packed in there, all of them on the second floor. Only one of them was actually working because there was only one game on the scoreboard. Sammy was in charge of Pirates-Yankees.

"We had a regular picnic."

"Shakes" was obviously thinking ahead. He found a spot for his high school guidance counselor.

No Yankees pitchers stopped in for a hot dog during the Series. Being American Leaguers, they weren't aware of what usually went on inside the scoreboard. I didn't ask "Shakes," but I'm guessing they would have been taken care of.

Since there was only one game posted on the scoreboard, guests had plenty of open windows to look through. As the game moved along, "Shakes" decided to change his vantage point.

"For the last three or four innings, I moved to the second-floor ledge.

It was a window on the side of the scoreboard that was located right above the left-centerfield wall. I could lean out and look right down the muzzle of home plate."

From his perch near the 406 mark, "Shakes" didn't get a real good look at Hal Smith's three-run homer in the bottom of the eighth that put the Pirates ahead 9-7. It went over the scoreboard and directly above his head. But nobody on the planet got a better look at Mazeroski's home run.

As everybody knows, Maz took Ralph Terry's first pitch for a ball.

He swung at the second pitch.

"I'm thinking it ain't getting out of here."

(Remember, "Shakes" had acquired a pretty good feel for when a ball was hit hard enough to clear that 406 mark from all his time inside the scoreboard.)

"My first instinct was that it wasn't going to clear. I looked at Yogi Berra and he wasn't moving very fast."

(Think of the millions and millions of people who have seen Yogi Berra watching that ball as he turned and headed for the leftfield wall at Forbes Field. "Shakes," because he had made the decision to move to the window, is the only guy on the planet who was able to watch Berra watching the ball.

"He had the same impression that I did — that it wasn't going out. I was coaxing that son of a bitch."

The other occupants of the scoreboard saw Maz swing and saw the ball heading for deep left-centerfield, but they had no way of knowing if it was going out.

"Everybody comes running toward the end of the scoreboard yelling, 'Is it gone? Is it gone?'

"I can't talk. The ball is 10 feet away. I heard it hit something on the way out — ivy on top of the wall or leaves on the tree. I thought that baby's not gonna make it."

"It just snuck out."

The Schenley Park Little League field was just behind the leftfield wall and that's where the most famous home run in history landed.

"It hits that sidewalk, just a big bounce. Mother of God, there must have been 200 people scrambling for the ball."

I don't know about you, but I'll never look at Mazeroski's homer the same way again. The scoreboard is prominent in every photograph of the home run, both moving and still, yet I never really paid a lot of attention to it.

Now every time I see Maz make contact, I'll have to think of those 20 people running along the second floor of the scoreboard yelling, "Is it out? Is it out?"

I'll also see the home run from "Shakes'" perspective: Looking right into Yogi Berra's face. And I'll think about the 15-year-old kid hanging out that window above that outfield wall, not far from where the ball disappeared.

Most people, when someone mentions Maz's home run, see the swing and Berra turning his back to home plate and watching the ball go over the 406 mark. When Dick Jeffers, better known as "Shakes," sees Maz's home run, he sees that ball floating only 10 feet away from him and remembers thinking, "That baby's not gonna make it."

"Shakes" worked in the scoreboard a few more years and saw a lot of great moments. He went to the last Pirates game played at Forbes Field in 1969 and watched, after the game, as the fans climbed the scoreboard like the Mexican army scaling the Alamo and ripped it apart, piece-by-piece.

"I'm glad my dad wasn't alive to see what they did to the scoreboard."

"That was sacred ground."

CHAPTER 29

YOU CAN'T CARE
MORE THAN YOUR BOSS

Long before I finally left the local TV news business there were signs along the way that things had changed for the worse and would never be changing back.

Two of them involved President George W. Bush.

Actually, the first time was when he was soon-to-be President George W. Bush. It was in August of 2000, the day after Bush's acceptance speech at the Republican Convention in Philadelphia.

The speech was well received and Bush's picture was above the fold on every newspaper in America. It was the topic on every talk show in the country. That morning Bush had boarded a train in Philadelphia and headed for Pittsburgh. It would be his first campaign stop after the speech — a pretty big deal.

You would think that Bush's appearance at Station Square on Pittsburgh's South Side that afternoon would be the slam-dunk lead story on the KDKA-TV five o'clock news.

You would be wrong.

I was interested to see where the story would play in our newscast because I had been noticing a dumbing down of the news for a several years.

George W. Bush didn't show up in the newscast until 5:30.

Oh, he may have appeared in some teases and bumpers, but the Station

Square story wasn't done until a half hour into the newscast. This was in the early days of the "BREAKING NEWS" era, when local stations everywhere were using that term several times an hour, so maybe there had been some "BREAKING NEWS" that pushed W back for half an hour.

Nope.

The big story on the 5 p.m. news that day was that it was the first day of the Three Rivers Regatta (sponsored, of course, by KDKA) and much of the first half of the newscast was devoted to promoting it. That was a pretty good sign that newscasts were now being presented for people who hadn't missed an episode of "The Price Is Right" since 1958.

The absolute final blow for me came a little over a year later. It was November, 2001. I had always wanted to do a story on the Army-Navy football game and I thought that because of the events of September 11 it would be the perfect time to do a story on a local kid playing at one of the two military academies.

There was a renewed sense of patriotism in the country then because of the terrorist attacks that killed almost 3,000 people and a renewed sense of appreciation for our military.

I contacted the Naval Academy's Sports Information Department and told them I would like to do a story on a local kid who would be playing in the Army-Navy game and they said they would get back to me with a recommendation.

A few days later I received a call from a woman on the academy's sports information staff and she gave me the name of a kid from Canonsburg who she thought would make an excellent story. She also promised that they would give me and our camera access to get shots of him in class, doing drills and practicing football.

It was exactly the kind of story that I loved to do — the kind that tells itself if you're willing to get out of the way. I learned early on that sometimes the less you involve yourself in a story the better it is.

KDKA cameraman Michael Challik and I had done some great work and won a few awards in the past — including the UPI award for best sports reporting in the country. It was the kind of story he loved, too. It was a no-brainer if there ever was one.

Or so I thought.

After I had received permission from the Naval Academy to meet with the local midshipman and we discussed the times and parameters of our coverage, I ran the idea past KDKA's News Director, Al Blinke.

He had no interest in doing the story.

My guess was that it didn't qualify as breaking news.

Keep in mind that there was a time when TV news directors and producers would have killed for a story like this. It was the kind of story that reporters were always encouraged to find. TV stations sought out reporters who showed the kind of enterprise and creativity that could produce this kind of story.

But in 2011 KDKA's newscasts are filled with video of vacant house fires in Butler County. And they wonder why the ratings continue to tank. I handled KDKA's decision the way I usually handled blatantly stupid management decisions. I shrugged my shoulders and repeated one of my former co-worker Bill Hillgrove's favorite sayings. "You can't care more than your boss."

A week and a half later, I turned on the Army-Navy game and almost fell off my couch.

I heard the announcer say something like this: "And the starting quarterback for Navy is senior Ed Malinowski. He's not the usual starter, but he has been such an exemplary player and model midshipman that the coaching staff decided to honor him by allowing him to start against Army."

This was no small thing. There may not be a more intense rivalry in sports than Army vs. Navy and Navy had decided that Ed Malinowski deserved a chance to say forever that he was the starting quarterback in the Army-Navy game.

I recognized Ed Malinowski as the name of the kid who Navy's sports information department had recommended as the subject for our story. But he didn't qualify as breaking news.

Malinowski played a couple of series at QB and gave way to the starter and Army won 26-17. But that wasn't the last I would hear about Ed Malinowski.

A few days later he was the subject of Dave Kindred's weekly column in the Sporting News. Kindred is one of the best sports columnists in the country and his column appeared on the back page of the Sporting News for years. He was in Philadelphia that day and wrote:

Such a glorious, sunny, summery December day in Philadelphia, Navy against Army, a day like no other day in college football history because of September 11, the commander in chief himself walking the grounds, making the game's coin toss after the Navy captain, Ed Malinowski called "Heads, Sir."

They'd met earlier, President Bush and the quarterback, when the president walked from Army's locker room to Navy's, thanking players for their service, promising them that in these days of war "we will prevail," and accepting from Malinowski a football signed by Navy's players, class of 2002.

As to how Ed Malinowski felt at the moment he handed the football to the president, he acknowledged the improbability of "a guy from Nowhere, Pennsylvania" presenting a football to "the leader of the free world." Then he said, "I was never more nervous."

I read the words "Nowhere, Pennsylvania" and all I could think of was Canonsburg and "BREAKING NEWS."

As I read Kindred's column, I pictured what a great story we could have done for KDKA. Who knows? We might have had enough access that we would have had a camera there when Ed Malinowski handed the football to President Bush or been allowed to videotape the tossing of the coin.

The kid from Canonsburg had made quite an impression that day. John Feinstein, who's written some of the best sports books in American history, including "A Civil War: Army vs. Navy: A Year Inside College Football's Purest Rivalry," says that if he could only go to one event in sports every year, it would be the Army-Navy football game. In a 2004 column for AOL.com explaining his love for the annual game, Feinstein wrote:

The nature of Army-Navy is best summed up by a brief moment three years ago when President Bush conducted the coin toss just 10 weeks after the tragedies of 9/11. When he tossed the coin in the air, Navy Captain Ed Malinowksi made the call on behalf of his team: "Heads, SIR!" he said, loud and clear for everybody in the packed stadium to hear. We all smiled at that moment because only at Army-Navy would you hear a future marine tell the President of the United States "Heads, SIR!" during the coin toss.

That would have been a local kid creating an all-time great television moment. While that coin toss was taking place, a KDKA cameraman was probably out getting pictures of a car accident, a dumpster fire or a dog bite.

Being the wise guy that I am, I made sure that the news director and the assistant news director saw Kindred's Sporting News column and I let them know that the Malinowski kid was the kid who was going to be in my story.

I also sent them an email that made several references to the fact that I realized that Malinowski's story didn't qualify as breaking news. Not long after I sent it, the assistant news director approached me in the newsroom with my email in her hand. She told me that she and the boss didn't appreciate my sarcasm and then suggested that I try to get an interview with Ed Malinowski. It was hard not to laugh in her face. I just mumbled something and walked away.

I worked at KDKA for seven more years, but I never suggested another story idea.

And what happened to Ed Malinowski?

Not long after playing in the 2001 Army-Navy game, he shipped out for the first of two tours in Iraq. In May of 2011, shortly after Osama Bin Laden had taken two in the eye from a couple of Navy Seals, Malinowski, who was working as a contractor for the Department of Defense, was interviewed by the Washington Post because he was a member of the Naval Academy's first post-9/11 graduating class.

Malinowski said, "Back then I can remember being hopeful. I was like, 'This thing is going to be over quick.' I was thinking I might not ever be involved in this, and then as things started moving on, and really not until I got to the basic school in 2003 and I'm going through Marine officer training there do I realize, 'Hey buddy, you're in the middle of this thing, and by the way we just invaded Iraq, and you're going.'"

He went and survived.

Twice.

I'm sorry I missed his story because it would have made for some really good television in what had already become a news wasteland, but I'm more sorry that I missed out on the honor of meeting the kid from Canonsburg, Ed Malinowski.

CHAPTER 30

SHORT STOP

IT MUST HAVE
BEEN THE 'STACHE

I don't think there is any debate over who is the best-looking player in Major League Baseball history.

It's Phil Garner and nobody is close.

And I don't say that because people used to tell me that I was a dead ringer for him.

In the summer of 1978 I was working for KQV Radio. It was a few months before I took the job at KDKA-TV that would make my face recognizable. I covered just about every Pirates home game that season and, after doing my post-game interviews, I would leave Three Rivers Stadium through the same exit that the players used.

Garner was the Pirates' third baseman at the time and a very popular player. He was short with a bushy red mustache. I can't count the number of times I was accosted by autograph-seeking fans as I came out of Three Rivers Stadium.

I would hear, "Hey, Phil, are you signing?" and I would say, "I'm not Phil. He's still in there."

The fans rarely bought the first denial.

I usually had to deny it two or three times as they were begging me for an autograph. More than once I took out my driver's license and that didn't always work.

I would still hear, "C'mon, Phil, just sign."

Why they thought Phil Garner would find it easier to flash fake ID than to just sign an autograph, I'll never know.

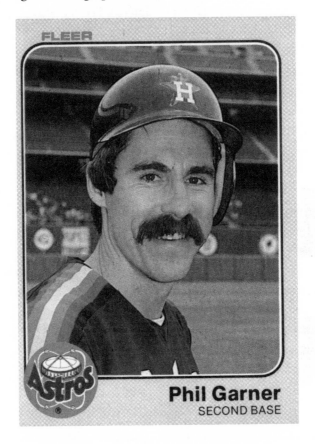

Phil Garner eventually came to realize that there was only room for one Yosemite Sam mustache in Pittsburgh and moved on to Houston.

One night, after a game that had been played in front of a big crowd, I was swarmed by 40 or 50 autograph seekers as I came out of the stadium.

No matter how strongly I denied that I was the guy they were looking for, they couldn't be convinced that I wasn't Phil Garner. I was actually backed up against a wall and was beginning to wonder if it was going to get out of hand. They didn't want to hear about a driver's license. They just wanted Phil Garner's autograph and some of the comments from the crowd were becoming pretty nasty — maybe even hostile.

I could have diffused it by signing Phil Garner's name, but I just couldn't bring myself to do it.

Just as I was starting to wonder if it was going to escalate into a problem, I was relieved to see Pirates General Manager Pete Peterson come through the exit.

"Pete, Pete," I yelled. "Over here. Will you please tell these people that I'm not Phil Garner?"

Pete looked me in the eye, looked at the crowd and said, "Aw, c'mon, Phil, why don't you just give them your autograph," and he walked away.

That really whipped the crowd into a frenzy. I finally escaped by inviting them all to follow me to my car, where I showed them my owner's card, which matched the driver's license that hadn't swayed them.

Somehow, these crazed people believed that Phil Garner would rather start a near riot by using fake ID than sign an autograph, but they weren't willing to believe that he would go to the extreme of riding around in a car with phony registration.

I hopped in my car and drove away and didn't — even for one second — consider shaving off the 'stache. Garner eventually shaved his but eventually came to his senses and grew it back.

He and I used to laugh about our resemblance all the time.

I don't remember him saying that he was ever asked for my autograph.

CHAPTER 31

PUT ME DOWN FOR A SIX
(ty-six)

ngelo Spagnolo had a 56 handicap at Linden Hall Golf Club in
Dawson, Pa.

Let's think about that for a minute. Par is 72. That means Angelo's average score was 128. There are people who would kill to average 128 in bowling. One of them is Barack Obama.

But this was golf.

That's more than seven strokes per hole.

Somehow, Golf Digest magazine, in June of 1985, found Spagnolo and three other guys and determined that they were the four worst avid golfers in America and, for some reason, decided that it was necessary to find out who was the worst of the bunch. They set out to find "America's Worst Avid Golfer."

Spagnolo, Jack Pulford, a restaurant owner from Moline, Illinois, Kelly Ireland, an attorney from Texas, and a stockbroker from Denver named Joel Mosser were set up to play each other at Sawgrass, the Tournament Players Club in Ponte Vedra, Florida.

Yep, *that* Sawgrass — the one with the island green on the 17th hole.

Since Angelo was a local guy, I thought that we (Channel 4) should cover it.

Back then, unlike today, news directors didn't buckle over in laughter or scream at you to get out of their office when you suggested covering a story that required spending more than a hundred bucks.

The news director, Joe Rovitto, saw the potential for a good story, so I was sent to Florida, along with a cameraman, to follow Angelo's attempt to lay claim to the title of "Worst Avid Golfer in America."

Remember, Angelo averaged 128 on a semi-private course in Fayette City, Pa. and this was Sawgrass, a course that chews up PGA players and spits them out.

Also keep in mind that in order for Angelo to average 128, he had to post some rounds in the 130s if not 140s.

It had the potential to be ugly.

The friendly folks at Golf Digest had no idea.

It was June and it was hot.

Florida Hot.

Florida Hot and Florida Humid.

Feels-like-a-hair dryer-in-your-face hot.

If you've never been to Florida in the summer, you don't know hot.

When the foursome was getting ready to tee off that morning, I couldn't help but notice that the official from Golf Digest, who was walking around looking really official with a two-way radio, was wearing a sports coat and tie.

For the first few holes it was funny watching the guys spraying the ball over the course, but it became apparent pretty early on that this was not going to end well.

It took more than three hours to get through the front nine and it was getting hotter by the hole.

It wasn't golf. It was four guys hitting golf balls with golf clubs but it wasn't golf.

I kept my eye on the guy with the sports coat and tie. Through nine holes, he was still wearing both and the tie was still nice and snug.

He was sweating a lot.

The big smile that he had early in the morning had disappeared after about three holes. He had to actually treat this fiasco like a real golf match and had to keep score and was clearly not having fun.

As the day went on, his officious, pompous manner made him look more and more like he was provided by the casting director for "Caddy Shack."

It's too bad all the snowmen these guys were putting up weren't the kind that could have cooled him off.

An eight was usually good enough to win the hole.

As I remember it, Angelo was only the third or fourth worst for most of the day, which ought to give you an idea of how bad these guys actually were.

By the time we got to 17, Sawgrass' famous island green, everybody was miserable and Angelo was in third place — second worst — and, if he was going to win the title, he would have to be spectacularly bad on the last two holes to catch Jack Pulford of Illinois.

We know Angelo was a 56 handicap. How bad would Pulford have to be to "win" the match?

I noticed that the Golf Digest guy still had his sports coat on and his tie hadn't been loosened.

Boy, was he sweating.

How much of a pompous asshole do you have to be to wear a sports coat and tie for six hours on a golf course in 90-degree weather? I figured he deserved to be miserable.

He couldn't have looked more miserable.

This had stopped being fun for him at least four hours ago. Instead of smiling at the ineptitude of Angelo and the boys, he was rolling his eyes and scowling.

Of course, Angelo's tee ball on 17 was a screaming line drive into the water, so he went directly to the drop area.

When you're regularly shooting scores in the 120s and 130s, chances are pretty good that you don't have a really good short game. All Angelo needed to do was pitch a 30- or 40-yard wedge over the water to get on the green, but all he could do was hit line drives.

Click-splash.

Click-splash.

Click-splash.

The *click* was the blade of his pitching wedge hitting the ball.

It may have been a pitching wedge but there was no pitching going on. We're talking hard line drives here.

Every line drive was a stroke and every drop was another stroke.

I was standing a few feet away watching every shot. I noticed that someone from Golf Digest (not wearing a sports coat) was handing Angelo a brand new ball from a sleeve of Pinnacles after every splash. (Pinnacle was the hot new ball for that season.) After 15 or 20 line drives, I noticed that the balls had a black line around them. He had started giving Angelo driving-range balls.

After 26 shots into the water, Angelo took out his putter and started knocking his ball up the walking path to the hole. The last putt on to the green was hit so hard that it came within a few feet of rolling off the other side and into the water.

If that had happened, Angelo would have been required to go back to the drop area and the guy in the sports coat would have beaten him to death with his pitching wedge.

We would have had tape at 11. *Exclusively* of course.

Angelo made a clutch putt for a 66 to take the "lead" in the tournament going to 18.

Think about how ugly it must have been *after* Angelo gave up and started putting the ball up the cart path. I think that alone took 13 strokes.

So, it's on to 18.

The sports coat is still on and the tie is snug and Mr. Officially Officious is visibly annoyed. He saw nothing funny about Angelo's 66 and he just wanted this bad idea to be over.

Angelo proceeded to hit his tee shot about 50 feet into some really tall grass in front of the green. Several officials were using golf clubs to separate the grass trying to find the ball.

Believe it or not, it was a lost ball and Angelo had to go back to the tee.

That was it for Mr. Sports Coat Man. He shook his head and stomped off to his golf cart. He jumped in and hit the accelerator pedal so hard that he almost suffered whiplash and made it clear to everybody that he was pissed off and couldn't take it anymore. He'd see us all on the 18th green.

Angelo stepped up to the tee and looked down the fairway that was protected by water on almost the entire left side. Mr. Sports Coat's cart was speeding up the right side of the fairway when Angelo swung.

It was a humpback liner.

BANG!

That's the sound that Angelo's ball made when it caught up to the back end of Mr. Sport Coat's cart 200 yards away.

Mr. Sports Coat never flinched and never looked back. He just kept the pedal to the metal and went to the 18th green.

It was a scene right out of "Caddy Shack."

Angelo's 66 on the par 3 Number 17 locked up the title for him but I'm pretty sure he finished with an 18 on 18.

His final score was 257. Pulford finished at 208, Mosser 192 and Ireland at 179.

How about that Ireland breaking 180?

The guy with the best score averaged just under 10 strokes per hole. If you play golf, you know how bad you have to be to get a 10 on any hole. Think about averaging 10 strokes a hole.

Then think about averaging 11 strokes a hole, which is what Angelo did for 17 of the 18 holes on the course.

Jack Pulford averaged 12 per hole for his round. I vaguely remember that he had a 30-something on 17.

The Players Championship at Sawgrass has become known as the "Fifth Major" on the PGA tour and Number 17 is one of the most famous holes in golf.

Every time I see the biggest names in golf making their way to the green on that walkway, I think of Angelo and all those brand new Pinnacles at the bottom of that lake.

And that sports coat and tie.

WHILE WE'RE ON THE SUBJECT

Take two weeks off and quit.

That was always my favorite piece of golf advice. Golf pros were known to say it when they were kidding one of their students. The students thought they were kidding, which they were, but only about 40 percent of the time.

I actually took two weeks off and quit 11 years ago and haven't played a round of golf since.

I quit because I had a bad knee and because I stunk. I knew, because of my knee, that I couldn't continue to take lessons and go to the driving range to try to get better, so I packed it in.

And I live on a golf course.

I quit cold turkey. By the time I packed it in, my handicap was about a 16. Up from a low of 13.

I think that's pretty respectable and probably better than 90 percent of the people who haven't taken two weeks off and quit yet.

Why is golf so hard for people to give up?

If you're a 56 handicap, isn't that a pretty good sign that you should be bowling?

Would the bowling equivalent of a 56 handicap be never being able to roll a 100?

Myron Cope and I were members of the same country club for about 15 years and he is still the worst golfer I've ever known. I'm pretty sure that Myron went to his grave having never broken 100.

Yet, he was always the happiest guy on the course.

The unhappiest people were playing behind him.

I never asked him why he kept at it because I knew the answer. He didn't really care what he shot, he just enjoyed being out on the course.

Someone once told me that in Holland, because of the scarcity of space for golf courses, players have to prove that they're worthy of playing by going to the driving range and being certified by a pro.

I've never been able to verify that, but it sounds like a really good idea to me.

There was a 36-handicapper in my country club who used to plumb-bob shots from 230 yards out. If I had been in charge, the penalty for that would have been dragging him face down behind a golf cart over the front nine.

Think about how much more enjoyable golf would be if only people who were actually capable of, you know, playing golf showed up at the first tee.

I could be talked into a federal ban on anybody who didn't break 100 on at least two out of every three rounds.

If you're out there shooting 110 on a regular basis, it's time to get yourself a really nice bowling ball with your initials on it, a really nice bowling ball bag and your very own bowling shoes.

You stink.

I'm not a bowler (although I did break 200 once), but I can't imagine that the bowling alleys are full of people who are rolling 47s and 56s.

How long would you stick with skeet shooting if you never shot a skeet? How about archery if you never hit the target?

So why do people who can't play golf continue to clutter up the golf courses?

(I'll bet a lot of them could be weeded out if you made it mandatory that they run after every shot once they've hit 95.)

If you're shooting 105 to 115 every time out, you don't really need golf clubs. You could bring garden tools and it wouldn't affect your score.

I'll bet there were guys at my old club who could have beaten Myron using a hoe and a pickaxe. Hell, there were a few who could have beaten me with a hoe and a pickaxe.

In golf, I mean.

Angelo Spagnolo seemed like a really nice guy, but would you want to be playing behind him on the one day of the week that you can play golf?

How about showing up at the first tee and discovering that Angelo will be joining your threesome?

CHAPTER 32

QUOTES FROM THE UNFAMOUS

My dad (Bill) was a good golfer. Actually he was really, really good — probably in the 98 percentile of amateur golfers. He carried a five handicap at Churchill Country Club. Someone who was visiting at our house spotted a golf trophy and asked my mother (Kay) what my dad had won.

"He didn't win anything," she answered. "That's for perfect attendance."

CHAPTER 33

TRIPLE SIX FIX

I remember my first sportscast for WTAE-TV.
It was Sunday, December 18, 1978. I had been working as sports director of KQV radio when I got a call the previous Monday from Myron Cope, who told me that his news director, Fred Young, was interested in talking to me about an opening for a weekend sports anchor. Myron used to listen to me on his way to work at WTAE radio, liked what he had heard and had put a good word in for me.

I did an audition on Tuesday, was called back for another audition on Thursday and offered the job immediately after that second audition. It all happened so fast and there I was three days later in the newsroom with no idea how to prepare a sportscast. I was pretty good at writing a script and reading it from a teleprompter, but I had no idea how to write a format for the show that would allow the director to know what I was doing.

Bob Reichblum, a 23-year-old desk assistant who would later become Executive Producer of "Good Morning America," held my hand and showed me how to do the official format.

I got through the six o'clock news without a hitch and I was on my way. The original plan was for me to only do the Sunday night show, but the bosses were so pleased with what I had done that they told me to anchor every night the following week. I went from doing morning and afternoon drive on KQV radio to doing the six and 11 o'clock news on Channel 4 in a matter of days.

The weeknight 11 o'clock sportscasts were a little more complicated in those days because of all the scores. It's hard to believe or understand why now, but back then we gave every score imaginable, including partial NBA and NHL scores.

Even then, I wondered about the value of giving a first quarter NBA score.

Lakers 4, Warriors 2 — 1st Qtr.

How does that information help anyone?

When you think about it, what's the point in giving the score of a baseball game that's in the third inning?

But scores were very important in those days.

In 1978 scores were done a lot differently. There was no digital way to put the scores on the screen. The white letters and numbers were attached to a large black drum. The stagehand on duty was in charge of sticking the letters and numbers on the drum. One of the studio camera operators would zoom in on the characters and they would be superimposed on the screen. The stagehand would slowly turn the drum, moving along from score to score as I read them.

I had to check the Western Union ticker several minutes before we went on the air to get the scores so that I could take them down to the studio and give them to the stagehand to put them on the drum.

I think I met Freddy Luman on my second day at Channel 4 — Monday, December 19, 1978. He was the stagehand that night and I couldn't believe how helpful he was. He would come down the hall from the studio and check the ticker two or three times an hour, so I didn't have to worry about getting the scores and he would stick the letters and the numbers on the drum.

During my first year and a half at Channel 4, I came to really appreciate Freddy because not having to worry about getting those scores made my job a lot easier and I could devote time to watching and editing highlights instead of the busywork of pulling scores from the ticker and running them down the hall to the studio.

I couldn't believe a guy would be so nice.

Then I found out why he was so anxious to get those scores.

Freddie was apparently booking bets while he was working at Channel 4.

That wasn't all that Freddie was doing on the side.

He was plotting to fix the Pennsylvania Lottery.

The mastermind was Nick Perry, who had been working as an announcer at WTAE-TV since 1958. He was the guy who called out the daily lottery numbers as the Ping Pong balls popped out of the state's lottery machine, which was located in WTAE's TV studio. Perry was also host of a show called "Bowling for Dollars" and was a well-respected TV personality. (The bowling alley was actually set up in the WTAE studio.)

Every night Perry saw those Ping Pong balls flying around in the drum, with the three winning balls being sucked out one by one, and he thought it would be easy to rig the daily numbers game.

And it *was* easy.

Perry went to WTAE-TV Art Director Joe Bock and asked him if he could replicate the balls being used in the Pennsylvania Lottery and make them heavier. Bock was willing to go along with the plan and he was able to weight the balls by adding latex paint.

The plan was to weigh down all the Ping Pong balls except the 6s and 4s. That would limit the number of possible combinations to eight — a pretty safe bet.

Perry also got state lottery official Ed Plevel, who oversaw the drawings in the studio every night, to leave the balls and the machines unguarded a few times.

Freddie "The Friendly Stagehand" Luman, who was in charge of setting up the lottery set each night, agreed to switch the weighted Ping Pong balls with the regular balls.

On April 24, 1980, at seven o'clock, millions of viewers and maybe millions of lottery ticket holders saw three Number 6 balls get sucked through the vacuum and heard Perry say the winning number was "Six, six, six."

Meanwhile, Perry's business partners in another venture, Pete and Jack Maragos, had traveled around the state and bought several thousand dollars worth of lottery tickets with the eight combinations of the numbers 6 and 4.

The 666 was the highest payoff in the history of the Pennsylvania daily number and the conspirators might have gotten away with it if not for Tony Grosso.

Grosso, along with being my future next-door neighbor in Mount Lebanon, was running Pittsburgh's illegal daily numbers game. He knew something was up because the Maragos brothers had told way too many people about the fix and Grosso saw that way too much money had been bet on those numbers. I remember hearing stories about Grosso calling KDKA-TV and radio and demanding that they report that the drawing had been fixed.

Grosso let it be known around town that his organization, which used the state's lottery number, wouldn't be paying off on 666. Eventually, Pennsylvania law enforcement agencies got involved and it didn't take them long to nab Perry, Freddie and the boys.

The phone records showing lots of calls from Perry's announcer's booth at WTAE to the Maragos brothers put enough heat on them to get them to testify against Perry.

I remember Freddie Luman looking very stressed out at the time and later heard stories that the cops had threatened to nail him for running his bookmaking operation out of the WTAE-TV building, which convinced him to also testify against Perry.

The Maragos brothers got two years in prison, Luman got less than that and Perry got seven. He served two before being released to a halfway house for a year. Bock received a light sentence in exchange for his testimony against Perry.

I was sentenced to getting those partial NBA scores for myself.

WHILE WE'RE ON THE SUBJECT

Thinking about those early days of working at Channel 4 got me to thinking about what a strange feeling it was for me that first week on the job in December of 1978.

I was thrilled to be working at KQV Radio and, at the time, thought that I would be satisfied with my career if I had stayed there for 30 years.

I had never applied for or shown any interest in getting a job at Channel 4. I think it was after a Chuck Noll press conference on Monday, December 12, when Myron Cope told me that because of a contract dispute between WTAE and their Monday-to-Friday sports anchor, Steve Zabriskie, Bill Hillgrove was moving from weekends to the weeknight job and there was an immediate and desperate need for somebody to anchor sports on the weekends. Cope told me that he had recommended me to WTAE news director Fred Young and gave me Young's number.

I called Young the next day and he asked if I could come out to the station that afternoon and do an audition. I told him that I could but I would have to do it wearing a sweater because that's what I wore to work that day at KQV.

Young said that would be OK and I went to WTAE in between my drive-time shifts at KQV and wrote and read a sportscast. Young thanked me and I left to go back to my radio job. The next day (Wednesday) Young called and asked if I could come back on Thursday and do another audition wearing a sports coat and tie.

I went out and bought a suit (I didn't own a suit or a sports coat at the time) and did my second audition.

I went from the studio to Young's office where I was offered a five-year contract and was asked if I could start on Sunday night. I was told that Hillgrove would be unavailable because he would be traveling with the Pitt football team to the Gator Bowl.

Believe it or not, Myron Cope was a backup sports anchor in those days and the plan was for him to anchor the 6 and 11 o'clock sports the rest of the week.

I wasn't as nervous as you might think that first night on the air and got through it without a hitch. When I came off the set after the 11 o'clock news, I got a call from Young and he told me that he wanted me to anchor the sports for the rest of the week.

In less than a week I had gone from being a sportscaster on a second-tier radio station to anchoring the sports on a station in one of America's top 10 markets.

I got an early lesson in the power of television that first week. I had agreed to give KQV two weeks notice after I accepted WTAE's offer, so after doing the sports on Channel 4 on Sunday night I was back up at 4:30 the next morning and headed into town for my morning-drive radio gig.

After my last sportscast at 9:15 a.m., I left the KQV studios on Seventh Avenue and headed for the parking garage down the street. The sidewalks were still pretty crowded and I was walking along in the middle of a good-sized mixture of people, all of us bundled up in winter clothes, when a guy coming toward me nods and says, "Nice job last night."

I was stunned.

Here I was, walking in a crowd of people on a busy sidewalk and this guy who had only seen me on TV for the first time no more than 15 hours before, was able to pick me out and critique me on my first performance.

That night things got really strange.

I found myself sitting on a news set with Don Cannon, Paul Long and Joe Denardo. Cannon had been doing the news on Channel 4 since 1969, but Long and Denardo had been around forever. I had been watching both of them since I was a kid.

It was almost an out-of-body experience.

It didn't take long for those guys to become simply co-workers and friends, but I'll never forget how strange it felt to be sitting next to them on December 19, 1978.

About 20 years later, after I had been working for KDKA for several years, I paid a visit to WTAE and the longtime receptionist, Irene Rabinowitz, told me, "I remember the first time you showed up here. After your audition, Fred Young called me into his office and said, 'You wanta see a guy who's a natural for TV?' and he played your audition tape."

If I had known that, I wouldn't have been so quick to sign that $23,000 contract.

CHAPTER 34

SHORT STOP

HOLY HOCKEY FIGHT

I have no problem with fighting in hockey. I also have no problem with people who have a problem with fighting in hockey. I do have a problem with people who become hysterical at the sight of a hockey fight.

Especially when it's a man who is hysterical.

Of course, the people who do get hysterical don't get hysterical as the fight is taking place. They usually do what everybody else does.

They glue their eyes to the hockey fight.

The hysteria comes when they write their newspaper columns or do their commentaries demanding that the NHL get rid of fighting.

The next time you see a hockey fight, check out the crowd and see if anybody is covering his or her eyes. Also, see if you can spot anybody who is sitting down.

Two athletic men in protective gear wailing on each other in the middle of an arena is a compelling sight. It's also a little sick, but I think that's what I like about it.

I used to love boxing (back when I knew who the fighters were) for the same reason. The barbarism is what made it attractive.

If fighting disappeared from hockey, I would still love the sport, but I'm happy to watch a good hockey fight anytime.

And how can you not love a sport that produces a Christmas card like the classic one sent out by the Penguins in the early '80s that featured one of their all time goons, Gary Rissling?

Rissling is on the cover sandwiched between a referee and a linesman who are trying to prevent him from pummeling an opposing player lying on the ice. Rissling has a wild, maniacal look on his face.

The caption read, "Peace on Earth, Goodwill Toward Men, Pittsburgh Penguins."

My favorite hockey fight took place at the Civic Arena in Pittsburgh on Wednesday, November 21, 1981. A little background:

The previous Saturday the Penguins had played the Canadiens in Montreal and their goon, Paul Baxter, got in a major brawl with the Canadiens' goon, Chris Nilan. It made big news when Nilan decided to get the last lick in by picking up a frozen puck in the penalty box and bouncing it off Baxter's head while he was sitting in the other box.

Baxter was cut but not seriously hurt.

This was pre-ESPN and YouTube, but the incident got as much coverage as the NHL could get in those days and from the moment it happened, the media and the fans started looking forward to the Canadiens game in Pittsburgh four nights later.

Baxter wasn't just a cement head. He was a solid defenseman and a very smart and well-spoken kid. The scars on his face made him look awfully mean, but he was also soft-spoken and very religious. You couldn't get through an interview with him without some reference to God.

We had access to players for our 6 o'clock live shots in those days and it was a no-brainer that I would interview Baxter before the game with Nilan and the Canadiens. Every hockey fan and sportswriter or sportscaster in town knew that the big story was going to be the first Nilan-Baxter confrontation after the puck-throwing incident.

Baxter wasn't about to feed the hysteria. I asked him what he had planned for Nilan the first time they were on the ice together and he played dumb and acted as though he didn't know what I was referring to.

When I reminded him that Nilan had bounced a puck off his head a few nights ago, Baxter said something like, "Oh that. That's in the past. I haven't given it a thought." When I tried to press him on whether he would be looking for revenge, I got, "No. I've prayed about it and I forgive him."

Think about how long it takes for a puck to hit the ice after the referee drops it on a face off. What would you say, a fourth of a second?

I remember watching the ref drop the puck and then immediately looking to my right. Paul Baxter had his gloves off and he was wailing away at Chris Nilan along the boards on the far side of the rink. Pretty soon they were both standing toe-to-toe throwing haymakers.

It didn't last long and the Baxter-Nilan fight would never be submitted as one of the all time great NHL fights. But because of what led up to it and because of what Baxter had said to me and a large TV audience about an hour earlier, it instantly became my all-time favorite.

CHAPTER 35

MERRY CHRISTMAS, BEANO

Beano Cook, if nothing else, is an original.

The same way that Myron Cope and Bob Prince were originals. There are some people who are so unique that nobody would have the balls to try to imitate them. Beano carved out a nice career for himself in the sports world by doing what very few people in radio and TV have been able to pull off — being 100 percent himself.

Beano didn't change the way he looked or the way he talked in order to get a job on national TV. He didn't have to because ABC and ESPN came to him. And after he took the job, nobody tried to change him.

Beano is also one of those guys who has always been able to say things and get a laugh when 99 percent of the guys on the planet would get a punch in the mouth for saying the same thing.

I started working with him in the early 1980s at WTAE-TV when he was hired to give his college football predictions. We never used the term "point spread," but Beano would do more than predict the winner. He would predict the scores and the bettor could easily figure out whether Beano was advising him to give or take the points.

News Director Joe Rovitto came to me and said that he wanted me to be creative and make Beano's picks something more than him sitting in a studio. He suggested going to different locations around the city and having Beano make his picks there. My idea for a location for the first week was pretty simple. Beano and I took a ride on the Mount Washington incline. As we were riding down the mountain, I said, "Beano, who do you think might be inclined to win this week?"

Not exactly Peabody Award-winning stuff, but it was only the beginning.

I decided to base the location of each segment on how Beano had fared in his prediction the previous week. Beano would pick four college games against the spread, with the score in the prediction as code for the point spread.

The first week, Beano went 1-3.

I decided to do our second week segment in a sewer. I went to the sewer in front of the house where I grew up because I knew nobody would bother us there and I knew from experience that all it took to remove the manhole cover was a pickaxe.

Beano and I climbed into the sewer and I started the segment by saying, "Beano, you went 1-3 last week. You have to do better than that this week or this whole idea is going to go down the drain."

Again, not something that you would submit to the Emmy competition, but a little more entertaining than Beano sitting in front of a camera.

My sessions with Beano escalated from there and eventually became some of the best work that I did in my 30-year career. Beano took the tapes with him to New York where he was working on ABC's college football telecasts and a couple of the big shots there said that they would like to hire me as a producer. I wasn't interested but I was flattered.

One of the things about producing good TV is that you eventually create a bar that has to be reached or surpassed every week and that puts a lot of pressure on you. We shot the location segments every Tuesday and I would start thinking about the bit immediately after I had the results of Beano's four picks on Saturday.

There were many Tuesday mornings when I woke up and had no idea what I was going to do, but the standard had been set and everybody was waiting to see if we could top the previous week.

There are a few segments that stick out in my mind:

After a 4-0 week, we went to Froggy's Bar and Grill near Market Square and sat in the middle of a large Downtown lunchtime crowd. With everyone chattering and clanging silverware, I said, "Well, Beano, four and oh last week. You're on a roll, who do you like this week?"

As soon as Beano opened his mouth, the room went silent and

everybody froze and looked at Beano in great anticipation. It was a takeoff on the E.F. Hutton stockbrokerage ads that were very popular at the time.

One of my favorite bits came on a Tuesday when I had drawn a blank and was desperately looking for inspiration. Beano was working for the Penguins at the time and I decided to give him a call and ask him if he had any ideas.

The receptionist answered and when I asked to speak to Beano, she said, "He's tied up right now. Can I take a message?"

"Just tell him I'll be there in half an hour to shoot our piece for the news," I said. The receptionist had solved my problem. I found a rope and headed for Civic Arena.

The piece was simple: I walk into the Arena, ask for Beano and the receptionist tells me that he's all tied up. I tell her that I have to see him to get his picks for the week and she reluctantly lets me through to the office. I open a closet and Beano is inside, bound and gagged. He was coming off a bad week and the idea was that somebody who had followed his advice wasn't happy.

I asked Beano for his picks and he gave them to me while he was gagged. Of course, you couldn't understand a word he was saying, but we put the scores on the screen as he mumbled.

"Thanks, Beano," I said, "see you next week" and I shut the door as he was begging me to untie him.

OK. One more and I promise it's the last one.

Beano had a bad week and I decided that we would take him somewhere to relax. We went to a local health club and sat in the steam room. Neither one of us was visible, but you could hear our voices coming from behind the fogged glass. I told Beano to forget about the slump he was in and to relax and make his picks.

Beano's voice can be heard coming from inside the steam bath but he's not visible. We superimpose the scores over the shot of the fogged glass as he goes through his picks. As I come out of the steam room wearing only a towel wrapped around me, I say, "Beano, I think this was good for you. You seem relaxed and I think you're gonna have a good week."

Beano, still not visible, says, "I think you're right. I feel great," and as he emerges from the steam room, he's wearing his usual frumpy grey suit and tie and carrying his ever-present clipboard.

I thought it was funny. Maybe you had to be there.

My favorite Beano Cook story didn't occur on the air.

It was in the early '80s and we had only known each other for a few months. Beano, who, as far as I know, has never owned a car, needed a ride to the WTAE-TV Christmas party at Churchill Country Club.

I offered to give him a ride.

With my wife Jeani riding shotgun, I pull up in front of his downtown apartment. Beano approaches the car, and Jeani, who is laying eyes on Beano for the first time in her life, says hello and starts to lean forward to allow Beano to get into the back seat.

Beano's first words to my wife are, "I can't sit back there. You're going to have to ride in the back."

Ninety-nine percent of the guys on the planet would never dream of saying that to a woman they had never met and if they did they would have the door slammed on their hand.

Jeani got in the back.

The three of us arrived at the club and started looking for a place to sit. There were three or four couples gathered around a table and the wife of the assistant news director, Frank Graham, was trying to seat everybody.

Frank was a nice guy but very serious and pretty stiff and his wife seemed to be just like him.

People are jockeying around and Mrs. Graham is saying, "Why don't you sit here and let them sit over there." Then someone else would say that they wanted to sit over here and why don't you sit over there and Mrs. Graham would try another suggestion.

This went on for a couple of minutes with nobody knowing where to sit and Mrs. Graham politely and kind of stiffly saying, "OK, then, why don't you two sit here and Frank and I will…."

Finally, Beano, who has never met any of the people at the table, bellows in his Beano Cook voice, "Hey, lady, it's not the invasion of Normandy. Just sit down."

We all sat down.

CHAPTER 36

MIGHTY, MIGHTY SAINT B'S

Pat Bruce and his teammates didn't know what to do when their team bus pulled into the St. Bernard's Church parking lot on October 1, 1961.

They couldn't do what they had been doing for as long as they could remember, which was a chant that began under their breath… "We're from St. Bs. Couldn't be prouder, if you can't hear us, we'll yell a little louder."

The chant would get increasingly louder as the bus made its way to a parking spot near the nun's convent.

By the time the bus stopped, the kids would be screaming at the top of their lungs and banging their helmets on the seats and the ceiling.

According to Bruce, "That was our way of letting the nuns know that we won again."

On that day 50 years ago, the St. Bernard's football team had lost.

For the first time in 93 games.

The story made it into the Pittsburgh Post-Gazette.

It was a long time coming but it happened — St. Bernard's of Mt. Lebanon finally lost a Catholic grade school football game.

The Bernies had a string of 93 league victories before St. Anselm's of Swissvale ended the string with a spectacular fourth quarter at Dickson Field in Swissvale yesterday. The score was 26-20.

Bruce remembers just dead silence on the bus.

St. Bernard's wasn't used to losing.

The Post-Gazette story erroneously reported that the streak dated back to 1949 — it was actually 1953.

(I may not get all the numbers right in this story because it was a long time ago and I'm getting most of my information from old St. Bernard Sunday Bulletins.)

The last official loss by St. Bernard's (it's actually St. Bernard, but nobody has ever called it that) was actually in 1953.

The Sunday Bulletin on December 15, 1957, had a story about the football banquet scheduled for that night:

St. Bernard Parish pays tribute tonight to its football team which once more, in the St. Bernard tradition, was champion this year in the Catholic Grade School League. During the past 12 years, St. Bernard teams have won a total of 82 games, tied three and lost one.

The one loss had been in 1953 to Resurrection and that ended a 30-game winning streak. It's hard to determine the exact record, so let's just say that St. Bernard's lost two football games from 1948 or '49 until 1961. (Three, if you count an exhibition loss to St. Cyril in 1958.)

Winning football games was a big deal at St. Bernard's and, you know what, nobody apologized for it.

St. Bernard's did this at a time when Pittsburgh was not used to winning football teams. From 1949 through 1961, Pitt and the Steelers *combined* had only 10 winning seasons. The Steelers were beyond bad and Pitt was barely mediocre.

Things have changed a lot in the last 50 years. Pittsburgh has become a football town — something it was not until at least 1972, and now it would almost be considered a sin for any kids' football team to be as good as St. Bernard's once was.

A team with that kind of record in 2011 would probably be investigated for child abuse. A team couldn't possibly be that good unless the kiddies were being mistreated in some way. Coaches would be accused of overemphasizing the importance of winning.

That's why I like the St. Bernard's story so much.

It's about good, old-fashioned winning.

No apologies.

We like winning so much that championships aren't enough. We'll only settle for undefeated seasons.

Not only that, St. Bernard's was about making kids tough.

Many of the fathers who sent their kids to St. Bernard's in the '50s and '60s had come back from World War II and/or the Korean War. They had to go from boys to men in a hurry.

On September 10, 1950, here's what appeared in the Sunday Bulletin under the heading "What Football Means At St. Bernard."

Football at St. Bernard is not merely a form of recreation; it is much more. Every person has certain fundamental problems to face in life. It makes all the difference in the world whether a person faces his problems honestly, with courage and intelligence, or tries to sneak around the problems of life... There is no place on the football field for the sluggard, the shirker, the coward, the scatterbrain, the dolt, the leaner, the quitter, the egotist.

Most of these faults are the result of pampering. In a football game, the opposing team is seldom inclined to do much pampering. Football is just clean, hard give and take.

What a training to face the stern realities of life.

We have a lot of fine boys in St. Bernard's School and our aim is to bring out all of the best in them. We saw what football did to the boys last year. (Undefeated championship team.) *The benefit was almost unbelievable. It is a pity that many boys are physically unfit to take part in the training. They are missing something, just on account of their physical handicap, they need most urgently. They are our problems. The real football boy is seldom a problem. He has learned to tackle problems.*

How do you think that would go over in 2011?

Toughening up boys? What we're they thinking?

That statement was written by the pastor, Father Joseph Lonergan, and if you think that was politically incorrect, wait until you hear what he said about the Boy Scouts. We'll get to that in a minute.

The St. Bernard's Streak is about so much more than football. It's about turning boys into men without apology. I don't know about you, but for years I've been getting the impression that our schools have been doing whatever they can to make boys more like women.

Let's not be too competitive.

Let's not have winners and losers because the losers' self-esteem will suffer.

Let's let everybody be on the team even if they don't really want to be on the team and let's let them play even if they stink.

At St. Bernard's, boys were expected to play football and Pappy Joe Lonergan wanted to hear a pretty good reason why you chose not to play.

The male teachers were not referred to as teachers. They were coaches. That's because they were hired first as football coaches and second as teachers. That seems ridiculous now when you're talking about a Catholic elementary school and 12- and 13-year-old boys, but it's consistent with Father Lonergan's attitude about football and the way it prepares boys for life. He considered football every bit as important as reading, writing and arithmetic.

Tony Mazzocco was the coach in 1950 and he set the tone that created the Streak. He understood what Father Lonergan wanted. He wanted a coach who instilled discipline and toughness and he wanted to win. "He didn't want you out there treating these kids like little angels or anything like that," Mazzocco told me.

Mazzocco's practices were not a lot of fun.

"They were tough. They were tough. But they loved it."

Father Lonergan paid for Mazzocco to take trips to Notre Dame in South Bend, Ind., so that he could learn from the coaches there and observe spring practice. Remember now, we're talking about Notre Dame and we're talking about a grade school football team.

Mazzocco also had a winter program that included wrestling and boxing. Kids were asked to put boxing gloves on and spar so that the coaches could measure their toughness.

Try that in 2011.

He says he never got one complaint from a parent.

This was the early '50s, long before mothers and fathers thought they were obligated to be at every one of their kids' practices.

Father Lonergan didn't like the Boy Scouts and he wasn't shy about letting his flock know it. He told Mazzocco to take the Scouts and make them do calisthenics and short-order drills to toughen them up. According to Mazzocco, "He thought their actions weren't what a boy should be doing and he thought the Boy Scout leader was kind of a sissy who didn't discipline the boys enough. If he had his way, he would have gotten rid of the Boy Scouts."

I was a student at St. Bernard's in the mid 1950s and I remember being well aware of Pappy Joe's feelings about scouting. I don't think too many kids wore their Scout uniforms to school.

On March 8, 1955, Father Lonergan stirred things up around the world when a parishioner sent a copy of the St. Bernard Sunday Bulletin to his brother, a writer for the military magazine, Stars and Stripes.

It included this column from Pappy Joe.

The scout fanatics wonder how we can be so cantankerous as not to become enthusiastic over the Boy Scouts. We like a boy who is all boy. If he is not a boy when he ought to be a boy, he will not be a man when he ought to be a man. The Boy Scout is about 20 percent girl. That makes him a little gentleman. But a gentleman is a generic man. He must be a man before he can be a gentleman. The Boy Scout program, even at its best, does not appeal to the boy who is all boy. A boy who is 20 percent girl may be gentle, but he is a hybrid. We like a thoroughbred.

The Stars and Stripes ran the column and it was picked up by news outlets around the world. Father Lonergan's assistant came to him and said that there were reporters asking for him to comment on what he wrote about the Boy Scouts.

Father Lonergan said, "Tell them I'm not talking because, if I do, I'll say something worse."

Imagine the traction that his column would have gotten if the Internet had existed in 1955. In 2011, he would be the lead story on "The O'Reilly Factor" and he'd probably get a call from the Pope.

Dan Conway, a Pittsburgh attorney who lives in Mt. Lebanon and still attends Mass at St. Bernard's, played on one of those undefeated teams in the late '50s. He says St. Bernard's was "Like West Point for young boys."

He remembers being one of the few 6th graders playing on the varsity team. St. B's won but not convincingly enough for the coach. "We had to do about a hundred sit ups. In a sense it was punitive, but there was always that prospect of excellence and it was amazing how often they delivered."

"Excellence."

Imagine that.

Imagine the outrage today if a coach asked — no, *told* — a bunch of 11-, 12- and 13-year-olds to do 100 sit-ups after a win.

Depending on your age, you may or may not be horrified by some of the "mean" things that were done to kids at St. Bernard's. And not just to the boys on the football team.

These boys knew that Father Lonergan
was interested in results, not excuses.

Nobody, least of all the parents, thought that discipline and tough love was mean. The parents who sent their kids to St. Bernard's in the 1950s knew exactly what went on there and that's why they chose to send them.

Bernie Powers, a former Notre Dame quarterback who played for Frank Leahy and backed up Johnny Lujack, was St. Bernard's coach in the mid

1950s. He's in his mid-80s now and his memory isn't what it used to be, but when I asked him to describe his practices, there was no hesitation.

"Educational."

I was expecting "tough," "hard" or "grueling," all of which they were, but the toughness was part of the education.

"The education was *through* the physical, not *by* it," Powers said. The unapologetic emphasis on winning was part of that education, according to Powers. "The winning record had an impact on the student body. We had so much pride."

"When Father Lonergan hired me," Powers said, "he said, 'I pay for performance. Not excuses.' " The message from Father Lonergan was pretty clear. He wanted the winning streak to continue.

Viewed in the context of the 21st century, what went on at St. Bernard's in the 1950s seems like a classic case of an adult taking youth sports too seriously. But this was during a time before the concept of playing sports only for "fun" had been introduced.

Unlike today, when so many sports are all about the parents getting to dress up the kiddies in full uniforms so that they can *pretend* to be on a team, back in the dark ages of the middle of the 20th century, if you took the time and the money to put together a football or baseball team and asked the kids to show up for practice, the object was to win.

And I've never believed that there are thousands of old men whose lives were ruined by the trauma of having to play football for St. Bernard's during their formative years.

It's just the opposite, in fact.

Dan Conway says, "When I was in the sixth grade, practice was a worry for me every day. We scrimmaged every day against the 8th grade. You had to get used to getting your ass kicked."

How many parents today would be interested in their kids getting used to having their asses kicked?

There were no moms and dads at St. Bernard's' football practice. Eleven-year-old kids had to fend for themselves. Their parents wanted it that way. They wanted their boys to be toughened up. No excuses.

*That's Danny Conway at left guard. It sure looks
like Father Lonergan is looking directly at him.*

Coach Powers says that on more than one occasion a player who was a
minute or two late for practice was sent home by Father Lonergan. Powers
would tell the kids that if they were late they would "Get a size 11 in the
wrong place." Father Lonergan wore size 11 shoes.

According to Powers, Father Lonergan wasn't afraid to use a white lie
to get his players fired up. "Before a game with Resurrection (the team that
beat St. B's in 1953), Pappy Joe made up a letter that he said came from the
Resurrection football team, with things like, 'Hough is a sissy' and 'Quietor
is a bum,' and he showed it to the team. We won 74-0."

Conway is 66 now and some of that St. Bernard's mentality has stuck
with him. "When I walk laps at South Hills Village, I still square off the
corners because, when we practiced at Wildcat Field in Mt. Lebanon, we
had to run to the corners when we did laps."

The St. Bernard's football team became so good that in 1956 it was
divided into two teams — the Blue squad and the Gray squad — and each
won division championships.

Jim Bruni was an assistant coach in 1956 and was offered a job at Joy Manufacturing at $335 per month. Father Lonergan kept him by offering him $350 a month for 10 months.

Bruni was in charge of "sixth grade operations." There were five classes of 50 kids in every grade at that time and the sixth grade intramural program included tackle football in full pads. The team that won the championship would play an all-star team made up of players from the other four teams, and when those sixth graders got to seventh grade, they knew the St. Bernard system and the coaches already knew who the good players were.

"Our quarterbacks changed plays at the line of scrimmage," Bruni says. "Most schools didn't do that."

Bruni, who would eventually take a pay cut to teach at Baldwin High School, where he eventually became principal, says Father Lonergan wanted to win but his main goal was always about teaching the kids.

And Bruni and the other coaches knew how serious Pappy Joe was about his football program. "In 1956, all the coaches were in the office listening to Don Larsen pitching his perfect World Series game for the Yankees. Father Lonergan came in, just looked at us and we got up and left."

Discipline.

Accountability.

Consistency.

The football mentality wasn't just applied to football. It permeated St. Bernard's school. The nuns provided the discipline. Today St. Bernard's enrollment is about 350. In the mid-1950s, in the same building, the enrollment was around 1,800. Despite over-crowded conditions that would be considered inhumane today, there were very few discipline problems. If a boy got out of line, he wasn't sent to the principal's office. He was sent to coach Bernie Powers' office.

At Father Lonergan's request, a highly organized lunchtime intramural program was created for the boys. Each class elected a captain for softball and football. The schedules and standings appeared in the church bulletin every Sunday. When I was 9 years old and in the fourth grade, I was elected captain of the 4-1-softball team. It was my job to pick the starting lineups and make the batting order.

How many nine-year-olds are given that kind of opportunity in 2011?

Other fourth graders from the three teams that were not playing that day were picked to be the umpires. At the end of the game, the home plate umpire reported the score to one of the coaches. (Male teachers were all called "Coach.")

I used to think it was a really big deal to see my class' record listed in the Sunday bulletin. If your team was bad, it was there for everybody to see.

4-1 was bad.

I can remember being very much aware of the fact that 4-1's touch football team was in last place and not liking it. (According to the December 22, 1957, Sunday Bulletin, our record was 3-8-2.)

"You reacted exactly the way Father Lonergan wanted you to react," Bernie Powers said to me. "Putting the standings in the bulletin was strictly him. It was his way to drive the kids to be better."

It didn't help our touch football team.

How about that? The results of those lunchtime playground football and softball games are still there for everybody to see?

And now they're in a book.

I was the captain of the 4-1-football team, too, if I recall. I must have had a lot of really bad players.

The St. Bernard coaches were in charge of supervising the lunch recess and sometimes it involved more than settling football and softball disputes.

Powers talks of sitting every day with Father Lonergan on the wall that separated the playground from the adjacent cemetery. They would make note of the young kids who looked like good football prospects and every once in a while, they'd spot two boys fighting.

"Get the 16s." Father Lonergan would say.

Sixteens, as in 16-ounce boxing gloves.

The two boys would be separated, handed the gloves and told to go at it.

With the entire student body watching.

Horrifying by today's standards, but perfectly understandable and accepted at St. Bernard's two generations ago.

Just as a point of reference, at my 10-year-old grandson's school, the boys aren't allowed to play with a football during recess.

Someone might get hurt.

"I'd fire who ever came up with that rule," says Powers.

Football wasn't the only way to teach kids to be self-reliant.

Picture a 10-year-old kid doing what little Danny Conway did when he was in the fifth grade. "I lived in Brookline, but my parents were building a house in Mt. Lebanon, so I went to St. Bernard's. I was an altar boy. I had to serve Mass at 6:30 in the morning on Monday, Tuesday, Friday and Saturday. I stood in the dark by myself and waited for the streetcar to take me to the church."

The Mass was said in Latin in those days, so the altar boys had Latin responses to make during Mass. "On Saturday's, I served Mass in the convent. Sister Edwin was very intimidating and insisted that we get our Latin right. It was just you, the priest and 15 nuns. Talk about pressure. After that, going for the bar exam was no big deal."

There are parents today who won't let their kids go to the end of the driveway to get the mail out of fear that they'll be kidnapped. Will those kids be as prepared for pressure and adversity as Dan Conway was when he took the bar exam?

• • •

Then there was Sister Mary Flavia.

She was in charge of the school cafeteria and she took it as seriously as a prison warden. If you were to get 100 people who went to St. Bernard's in the 1950s to sit down with a sketch artist and come up with a composite picture of Sister Flavia, you would end up with a picture of the wicked witch in "The Wizard of Oz."

At St. Bernard's there was no large cafeteria where 1,800 kids could eat their lunch, so a complex system was devised that would efficiently allow kids to get their food and safely and quietly return to their classrooms to eat. (The nuns referred to lunch as "dinner" for some reason. I never did figure that out.)

A lunch ticket for the school cafeteria cost 25 cents and Sister Flavia was always concerned about turnout. I can remember sitting in class and hearing her rosary beads banging together (the Sisters of St. Joseph nuns wore enormous rosary beads on their waists) as she swooped into our classroom unannounced.

Sister would interrupt the teacher and say, "How many of you children are eating in the cafeteria today? Show me by holding up your cafeteria ticket."

If you carried your lunch that day, it was a moment of terror because she would get in your face and ask you why you were not eating her delicious culinary creations.

"I don't like chili con carne" was not a good answer.

(Sister Flavia's most popular dish was "Hot Roast Beef Sandwiches." She took a piece of Wonder Bread, dumped an ounce and a half of ground meat on it and smothered it with gravy that looked like motor oil.)

If you were a cafeteria customer, it was a good idea for you to eat all of your lunch — including the vegetables.

Sister Flavia would stand by the big wastebaskets and intercept any kid who tried to throw away any of those nasty canned green beans. There were tables near the wastebaskets where the kids she caught could be seen sitting and staring at their beets or various kinds of canned vegetables.

They would sit there until recess was over, if necessary.

Inevitably, kids would try to put one over on the good sister and try to hide the fact that they didn't eat their vegetables. It was usually the first or second graders who hadn't figured out yet that they couldn't get away with hiding the nasty stuff in their milk cartons.

Sister Flavia, probably through divine intervention, was able to detect a vegetable smuggler from 50 feet away. As they would get ready to dump their milk carton in the wastebasket, Sister would snatch it from their hands and shake it.

If there were green beans or peas or corn or lima beans in there, she would dump them out on a plate and tell the poor victim to go into a special room and eat them.

If you didn't want to eat green beans, soaking them in milk wasn't going to make you any more likely to eat them.

The room where the vegetable violators were made to sit had a large window that looked out on to the playground. I can remember looking in that window and seeing kids sitting in front of all types of vegetables with tears streaming down their faces.

The rules were the rules.

Dan Conway says, "I don't eat lima beans to this day. I was trying to hide them in my milk carton and she caught me and made me eat them with the milk."

To this day, I can't eat stewed tomatoes for the same reason.

My mother still reminds me of the time that I came home with sweet potatoes (which I still can't eat) in my shirt pocket. I was wearing a sweater and I figured Sister Flavia would never think to look in my pocket. Pretty resourceful for an 8-year-old kid, I'd say.

Keep in mind that Conway laughed when he told his lima bean story.

He wasn't traumatized by it. And I don't think there are thousands of St. Bernard's Baby Boomers out there who were traumatized by having to deal with Sister Flavia every day.

Also, keep in mind that our parents heard all the horror stories about Sister Flavia, but they didn't call Father Lonergan or the principal or the Pope and demand that she be banished to the church bell tower. Today, she'd be good for a segment or two on "The O'Reilly Factor," but she wouldn't last one lunch hour at any school in America.

• • •

Many of the things that went on at St. Bernard's that seem so horrifying by today's standards were simply accepted as things that you had to deal with. Your mother wasn't there to help you fool the mean sister. Your dad wasn't there to make sure that you got to play your favorite position on the softball team. You were on your own. It wasn't evil. It was well intentioned. And you know what?

It worked.

I feel pretty fortunate to have been taught in grade school and high school by teachers who had devoted their lives to teaching me. At both of the grade schools that I attended, most of my teachers were nuns who taught me during the day and went to the building next door and prepared the lessons for the next day. They lived to teach me. Same with the Christian Brothers at South Hills Catholic High School. They weren't perfect. But they were pretty damn good at getting their message across and you learned in spite of yourself.

Bernie Powers makes no apologies for the St. Bernard's football dynasty or any of Father Lonergan's methods that he was charged with implementing. His eyes welled up with tears when he said, "I never had a fearful moment. I never had a moment he wouldn't be proud of."

Tom Mackey was the quarterback of the St. Bernard's team that ended the winning streak in 1961. He says he remembers being well aware of the streak at the time, but he doesn't remember receiving any grief from anybody when it ended.

"It was the least important thing and the most important thing at the same time. To me and my teammates, it was the most important thing. To my parents and even my Uncle Bernie (Powers, who by then had moved on to coach South Hills Catholic), it was the least important thing. And never once did the guys who came before us in the football program ever say anything critical."

The St. Bernard's program produced plenty of great high school and college football players. Mackey went on to have a good career as a quarterback at South Hills Catholic and Edinboro. Those tough practices at Wildcat Field may have had something to do with Don Gmiter doing a pretty good job against Michigan State in 1966.

Gmiter was Notre Dame's tight end in one of the most famous college football games ever played — when Notre Dame and Michigan State tied 10-10. It was Gmiter's job to block Michigan State's Bubba ("Kill Bubba Kill") Smith, the most feared defensive lineman in football.

But that was no tougher than going against Rich Machel every day. Machel, who went on to become a star linebacker at Kentucky, is widely considered the best and toughest player ever at St. Bernard's.

Ernie Lewis, who played for St. Bernard's in 1960, went on to play running back at the University of Cincinnati, where he was in the backfield with the Number One pick in the 1969 NFL Draft, Quarterback Greg Cooke of the Cincinnati Bengals. Ernie also shared a Back of the Week award with O.J. Simpson during the 1968 season.

Ernie's quarterback at St. Bernard's was handing off to a more famous back in 1969. Dan Darragh was the Buffalo Bills quarterback when O.J. showed up as a rookie. (O.J. might not be where he is today if Father Lonergan had gotten a hold of him.)

Denny Phillips became a high school All American at Mt. Lebanon in the mid-'50s and went on to play for Notre Dame and the Steelers. Gene Breen also went to Notre Dame and spent seven years in the NFL as a linebacker, including a season in Green Bay with Vince Lombardi, who probably didn't scare him as much as Sister Flavia did.

But the football dynasty and the football players produced by St. Bernard's aren't why I thought this story was important. I think it's important to remember that there was a time when kids — especially boys — were put in a position where they could fail. When they were allowed to fight their own battles and face the consequences of their actions. When they were allowed to be boys. And I worry about the feminization of America that is taking place in our schools.

No football.

No dodge ball.

No tag.

Girls get to play, too.

On Sunday, December 22, 1957, the St. Bernard Church Bulletin contained a story about the football banquet that had been held the previous week.

Attorney James McArdle gave the principal address. "The Importance of Contact Sports" was the theme. This is especially important when so many fathers are occupied with matters other than the training of their children, paving the way for a matriarchal society, he said.

Mr. McArdle addressed himself to the boys with this advice:

"Don't be misled by the name Champion. A champion is only one who sets a mark which others try to best. A real champion develops a 'stick-to-itiveness' and the ability to stay in good shape. The victory was not won at Canton (St. Bernard had gone to Canton, Ohio and beaten the best grade school team in the state that season.) *but at scrimmage on a hot August day. This is the lesson which must be learned."*

There are hundreds of old guys like Dan Conway out there who came away from St. Bernard's toughened up by the discipline and self-reliance that was required to get through the school day and those afternoon practices.

But there was one thing that Conway and hundreds of other football players never learned at St. Bernard's.

"I never experienced a loss. That's pretty amazing."

And exactly what Pappy Joe had in mind.

ACKNOWLEDGEMENTS

Thanks (Again) to my brother Bill, the real writer in the family, without whom this book would not exist. (Again) to Jim Wexell, author of "Steeler Nation," whose advice and encouragement convinced me that I had at least one book in me. To The Senator John Heinz History Center, a great source of information for the chapter on Sam Brady, Pittsburgh's baddest man ever. To Mike Lazorko at WTAE-TV for finding long-lost videos in the Channel 4 archives. To Mike Vucovkan for finding the not-quite-as-long-lost videos at KDKA-TV. To Dick "Shakes" Jeffers for remembering all those stories from inside the scoreboard at Forbes Field. To MaryAnn Bradley for allowing me to borrow every St. Bernard's Church Bulletin from 1949 to 1961. To my friend Pat Bruce for his Internet wizardry. To my mother Kay for being Chief of the Grammar Police and my wife Jeani for putting up with me for 37 years.